lino tagliapietra

from Murano to Studio Glass | works 1954-2011

edited by
Rosa Barovier Mentasti
and Sandro Pezzoli

Marsilio

lino tagliapietra

from Murano to Studio Glass
works 1954-2011

Venice, Istituto Veneto
di Scienze, Lettere ed Arti
Palazzo Franchetti
19 February - 22 May 2011

promoted by

 IstitutoVeneto
diScienzeLettere
edArti

 CIVITA
TRE VENEZIE

with the contribution of

 REGIONE DEL VENETO

main sponsor

SCALETTA
di
VETRO

sponsors
Becky and Jack Benaroya
Paul and Roberta Bonanto
Cecilia Chung and Tony Leung
Bonnie Marx and John Laing
Susan and Mark Mulzet
Jim Schantz and Kim Saul

under the aegis of

PROVINCIADIVENEZIA

CITTA' DI
VENEZIA

in collaboration with
Venezia Iniziative Culturali srl

ISTITUTO VENETO
DI SCIENZE, LETTERE
ED ARTI

President
Gian Antonio Danieli

Vice-president
Manlio Pastore Stocchi

Academic secretary
Class of Moral Sciences,
Literature and Arts
Gherardo Ortalli

Academic secretary
Class of Physical, Mathematical
and Natural Sciences
Andrea Rinaldo

Administrator
Lorenzo Fellin

Director-Chancellor
Sandro Franchini

Organisation
Bruno Bertaggia
Antonio Metrangolo
Giovanna Palandri
Sebastiano Pedrocco

CIVITA TRE VENEZIE

President
Emanuela Bassetti

Board of directors
Fabio Achilli
Giorgio Baldo
Emanuela Bassetti
Giuseppe Costa
Gaia Morelli
Alberto Rossetti
Albino Ruberti

General Secretary
Silvia Carrer

Organisation
Francesca Gennari
Stefania Stara

Exhibition and catalogue
curated and edited by
Rosa Barovier Mentasti
Sandro Pezzoli

General exhibition
organisation and services
Civita Tre Venezie
Silvia Carrer
Stefania Stara
Francesca Gennari

Exhibition and installation
design
Silvano Rubino

Exhibition graphics
Gruppofallani s.r.l.

Press office
Sara Salmaso,
Marsilio Editori

Anna Zemella,
Istituto Veneto di Scienze,
Lettere ed Arti

Insurance
D'Ippolito & Lorenzano
Synkronos

Shipping
Dei Rossi Shipping

Acknowledgements
The curators wish to thank
Lina Ongaro Tagliapietra
Bruno, Marina and Silvano
Tagliapietra
Cecilia Chung
and all the lenders

LinoTagliapietra wishes to
thank
Jim Schantz
Kim Saul
Erik Demaine
Martin Demaine
and Stephen Powell

The Istituto Veneto di Scienze, Lettere ed Arti, one of the most prestigious cultural institutions in Veneto, has for some years been focusing special attention on the art of glass and the Venetian masters who, through their exceptional creativity, backed up by their skill in working the glass hot, have made Murano glass without equal in Italy and around the world.

Glass in some ways represents a paradigm of the creativity of the Veneto people, capable of joining the strength of their imagination and innovation to craft works that, precisely because of their extraordinary quality, take on the value of works of art.

So I greet the exhibition the Istituto is holding on Lino Tagliapietra with satisfaction. He is one of the most important figures in international glass art, capable of making blown forms of a delicate elegance using the most complex decorative techniques of Venetian tradition to achieve absolutely modern effects.

Starting from his manual experience gained as a workshop garzone at a Murano kiln, Lino Tagliapietra has been able to develop his technical skills and creative capacity, concentrating on the design of vases and lamps. This has brought him not only artistic and business success, but also a prestige that has led to him being requested for teaching work around the world, and more and more often in the US, where he has now opened a studio in Seattle, allowing him to continue his artistic work and divide his time between there and Venice.

So it is no mere chance that his vases and glass installations are on display in the most important European and American museums, such as the Victoria and Albert in London and the Metropolitan in New York, thus making him a promoter of the values, artistic abilities and economic production of our region.

Hon. Marino Zorzato
Vice President - Councillor for Culture
Regione del Veneto

The Istituto Veneto di Scienze, Lettere ed Arti intends this exhibition of work by the Murano master Lino Tagliapietra to be a fitting tribute from Venice to a grand master of the art of glass. His genius and absolute mastery of the glass technique have allowed him to create new and captivating forms and to revive ancient production techniques, resulting in works of an extraordinary beauty and elegance.

The Istituto Veneto here once again takes up the thread of its commitment to the sector of art glass, begun in the first decades of the 19th century and revived with new enthusiasm in 2004 to mark the opening of the Palazzo Franchetti. Glass exhibitions have been held regularly in recent years as part of a long considered project to highlight glass art, seen also in the context of Venice's social and economic life.

The Istituto Veneto is particularly pleased that this first solo exhibition dedicated by Venice to the master Tagliapietra is being held in the same rooms where the city paid tribute to another great Venetian artist, Zoran Music, at the start of 2010.

Along with the other leading Venetian institutes of advanced education, the Istituto Veneto di Scienze, Lettere ed Arti is part of a network of places where the spirit of a city, which must continue to welcome, support and promote the highest art in all its expressions, is recognisable and fortunately still recognised.

Gian Antonio Danieli
President
Istituto Veneto di Scienze, Lettere ed Arti

Photographs
Francesco Allegretto
Russell Johnson
Roy Charles White

translations
David Graham

front cover
Lino Tagliapietra
Angel Tear, 2011

© 2011 by Marsilio Editori® s.p.a.
in Venezia
first edition: February 2011
isbn 978-88-317-08173

www.marsilioeditori.it

Contents

lino tagliapietra

from Murano to Studio Glass | works 1954-2011

History, Tradition and Innovation in the Glass of Lino Tagliapietra

Rosa Barovier Mentasti

Lino Tagliapietra is one of the leading glass artists at an international level and undoubtedly now recognised as the most important representative of the Murano tradition around the world. The history of his family has been closely tied to the history of Venetian glass for almost a century. The brothers Lino and Silvano Tagliapietra in particular, both driven by a passion for glass, expressed in equal measure but in different ways, have made an extraordinary contribution to the promotion of Murano's glass heritage.

Lino in the Rob Adamson's Glass Eye studio, Seattle, 1981

Albino Tagliapietra, Lino and Silvano's father, determined the glass destiny of his sons, though certainly without foreseeing their success, by moving to Murano from the nearby island of Burano in 1926, shortly after Silvano, the elder brother, was born. In Murano Albino found work in the workshops of the Venini glassworks, and his younger son Lino was born in Murano in 1934. After various work experiences, Silvano (1926 – 2003), a genuine self-made man and versatile autodidact, became the director of two prominent glassworks on the island and promoted Murano production abroad, also in a freelance capacity. Alongside this, most of his time was devoted to the *Muran Nova* association and the periodical *La Voce di Murano*, a revival of a 19th-century publication. The association, founded in 1963, and the magazine, published from 1965 to 1979 - Silvano was its editor for a decade - was aimed at reawakening the civic sense of the Murano people and pride in their ancient glassmaking tradition. Silvano Tagliapietra was also the author of a series of books entitled *Cronache Muranesi*, stories about life on the island from the 18th to the 20th century, peopled by glassmakers and various personalities and told with good-natured irony.

Lino and Silvano Tagliapietra always felt themselves to be authentic Murano locals, integrated into the island's social fabric like few others, despite not being born into a family of ancient glassmaking traditions. On the other hand, the Murano glassmaking world has been kept alive over the centuries by its flexibility and by contributions of new energy from outside. The main figures in the history of glass in the 19th and 20th centuries included figures from relatively recent families, like the Moretti, the Zecchin and the Martinuzzi, new families, like the Salviati, the Camerino and the Venini, and very new ones like the Tagliapietra. In the Renaissance, too, when there were harsh restrictions against 'foreigners', one of the most successful glass masters and entrepreneurs was Giorgio Ballarin, who had arrived in Murano as a destitute immigrant from Dalmatia; and in 1527 the Venetian state recognised the inventor of *filigrana a retortoli* (twisted filigree), one of the most important glassmaking techniques, as Filippo Serena, who worked on the island but was originally from the Bergamo area.

Although very closely tied to Murano, the Tagliapietra brothers, in other ways very different, always shared an inclination that was fairly rare among the Murano people of their generation: the desire and ability to look beyond the confines of the Venetian lagoon and of Italy and to adapt to different environments. Silvano, with his wife Etta Ferro, cultivated a love of France, which was the destination of trips for business and for cultural and study purposes, and he even helped support the launch of the Vannes-Le-Châtel glass school. Similarly Lino, accompanied in all this by his vivacious wife Lina Ongaro, has explored the American continent both materially and culturally, and drawn stimulus from it for the greater creative audacity that has accompanied his development as a glass artist.

Lino Tagliapietra is primarily an artist of extraordinary creativity and, thanks to his strong character, has developed his own very personal style, which is recognisable even to the less trained eye and has exerted considerable influence. But Lino was born and remains a master glassmaker in the most noble sense of the term, and this influences the methods and results of his work as an artist. He was taught and has taught himself the glass art in light of the particular Venetian sensibility to glass, aimed at appreciating its characteristics as an absolutely unique material that can be melted, blown and moulded when hot. Indeed, glass is not seen as a surrogate for precious stones, rock crystal in particular, as is the case in some other glassmaking centres with different historical traditions, and consequently engraving and cutting have a less important role in his pieces than hot working. In his work it is also difficult, if not impossible, to separate the design stage from the technical-experimental, in that he thinks in glass; that is, he conceives the work not only in terms of its aesthetic qualities but simultaneously in the methods of its production. Furthermore, at times glass forms and fabrics spring from technical experimentation, even from unexpected and erroneous results, set aside for some time then rethought, at others the initial design evolves during the course of its production.

Before attaining the privileged role of creator and maker of his works, Lino Tagliapietra climbed the usual hierarchical ladder of the Venetian glassworks. This is a kind of *cursus honorum*, codified since the middle ages, ranging from the role of the *garzonetto* at the lowest level to that of the *maestro* at the peak of his career. The young apprentice moves into glassmaking by getting practice in the preparation of the *pontello* for the master, helping in the moulding of the blown glass like a surgeon's assistant, until he has learnt the methods used to make the stem and bowl of a goblet and a vase in its entirety and, finally, coordinating the work group known as the *piazza*. It is a pathway in which nothing is taken for granted. Not all the *garzonetti* and *garzoni* actually have the natural predisposition and the strong will needed to acquire the technical skill and authoritative competence of the genuine master. Lino was evidently predisposed to this work and was also gifted with passion and tenacity. The person in a glassworks able to master all the techniques and to make all the models, from the goblet to the vase, from the chandelier to the sculptural form is traditionally known as the *primo maestro*. At a time when specialisation is to the fore, the *primi maestri* are disappearing, but Lino Tagliapietra can claim this title for himself.

In the course of his career, a master glassmaker aims at perfecting his manual skills and studies with daily practice until he achieves absolute symmetry of perfectly balanced forms and faultless regularity of the glass fabrics, for example filigrees. Such balance and regularity obtained with sure, deliberate movements and with apparent ease are much more appreciable in the moulding of an incandescent, fluid and, in its own way, rebellious material. Once he has reached this level, the master can allow himself anything. He can move away from the symmetry of the forms, but not because of any lack of ability; he can create glass fabrics of an entirely contemporary, or apparently casual, graphic impact. This extraordinary casualness, which certainly must not be mistaken for the approximations of those glassmakers who have not acquired complete mastery of the techniques, is recognisable in the making and in the final product and can be defined with an unusual term of Renaissance origin: *sprezzatura* (nonchalance). This term was coined by Baldassarre Castiglione, the author of *Cortegiano*, an instruction book for the courtier in the highest sense of the term: the educated and elegant companion of the prince, who best embodies the ideals of life at the time. He, says Castiglione, must '*fuggir quanto si po, e come un asperissimo e pericoloso scoglio, la affettazione; e, per dir forse una nuova parola, usar in ogni cosa una certa sprezzatura, che nasconda l'arte e dimostri ciò che si fa e dice, venir fatto senza fatica e quasi senza pensarvi. Da questo credo io che derivi la grazia*' (avoid affectation as much as possible, like a dangerous, rugged rock; and, perhaps to use a new word, in every thing assume a certain *nonchalance*, which conceals art and makes it seem that what one does and says is done without effort and almost without thinking. I think that grace is derived from this). The author adds: '*si po dir quella esser vera arte che non par esser arte*' (it may be said that real art is that which does not seem art). Castiglione obviously intends art here in the broad sense of the term, that is, every activity governed by rules and based on study and experience, and considers in first place the art of one's behaviour in social life, which must be marked by the utmost naturalness or *sprezzatura*. The author then also highlights this quality in relation to painting, music, dancing and riding. How can the creative freedom and executive assurance of Lino Tagliapietra and other grand Murano masters of a not distant past - primarily Alfredo Barbini and Archimede Seguso - not be equated with Renaissance *sprezzatura*? Anyone who has seen them work cannot but agree with Baldassarre Castiglione.

While he was acquiring the natural way of working that is typical of the great masters, Lino Tagliapietra was developing a highly personal style in the creation of works based on his own design. This development, which took place over several decades, was accompanied and stimulated by instruction, significant meetings, travels, considered or chance decisions and even lost opportunities. The extent to which such circumstances positively influenced Lino Tagliapietra's career has depended primarily on his own audacity, his openness to stimulus, his sensitivity and his intelligence.

Lino began working in a glassworks very young, having refused to continue his studies at the age of ten

Lino working in Paris watched
by his brother Silvano, on the
occasion of the exhibition
Ricordando Etta, in memory of
Etta Ferro Tagliapietra, at the La
Différence gallery, 1993

Lino working a plate in the La
Murrina glassworks, 1976

against the will of his parents, perhaps encouraged by the fact that at that time many of his Murano companions joined the world of work at an early age. It was 1945. After a short period at Giuseppe Toso's glassworks, one of the numerous glassmakers of the ancient and widespread Toso family, he worked as *garzonetto* in the *piazza* of 'Piccolo Rioda', an independent *maestro* who, along with his associates, rented work space in various glassworks. After Rioda he went to the Archimede Seguso glassworks, where he was taken on in 1946 at the age of eleven. Leaving aside any consideration regarding child labour in the glassworks, still normal practice in the mid 20th century, the start of Lino Tagliapietra's career could not have taken place in better circumstances. Indeed, after the second world war Murano enjoyed an exceptionally prosperous and creatively dynamic period. In the enthusiasm of the postwar economic recovery new companies were being set up, some of which aligned themselves with the most celebrated historical glassworks in terms of quality of production and commercial success. The number of *piazze* in the glassworks multiplied, each one coordinated by a master with specific skills, such that the production range was more varied than ever. Numerous designers and artists came to Murano, keen to take up the challenge of design in the glass sector, ensuring instantaneous stylistic updating. The Murano proposals, presented at the Biennali in Venice and the Triennali in Milan, were distinguished by an exceptional originality both in terms of aesthetics and technique, and developed essentially along two lines. Some glassmakers and designers concentrated on the creation of sculptural forms in solid glass worked hot, an absolutely recent sector, begun in Murano around 1930. Others focused on reviving the most refined techniques of Renaissance glass, blown very thinly and boldly modernising it to incorporate the decorative and chromatic vibrancy of the 1950s.

Both these trends were followed in the Archimede Seguso glassworks, which took Lino Tagliapietra on as *garzonetto*. The company had been set up in 1945 by Archimede Seguso, formerly master and partner of Seguso Vetri d'Arte, where he had become renowned as an extraordinary designer and maker of solid figurative sculptures, which remained his speciality throughout his long career. At the same time he began formulating very refined blown glass pieces based on ingenious innovative variants of the ancient filigree technique, the *Merletti*, for example; thanks also to the input of the master Enrico Moretti, whose glassmaking merits have never been pointed out. It is easy to imagine the very young Lino, introduced into a crowded and certainly not easy environment, trying to adapt to the rhythms of the work and looking around him, perhaps more interested in the human talents and charisma of the masters than the artistic qualities of their work. Yet it seems that subconsciously he made a choice between the various production sectors in favour of the light and essential filigree blown glass, almost undergoing a vague 'imprinting' whose signs were to emerge in his maturity. He stayed with Archimede Seguso until 1955, apart from a break for military service, but it was not here that he was to discover his vocation for glass making and feel that he had potential.

In Murano family ties - that is, linear, transverse and acquired relationships - very often determine the composition of the companies and also favour various kinds of working relationships. At times the end of such relations causes deep family ruptures. Lino Tagliapietra made professional choices based on family ties on a good two occasions: his more than ten years working with the Galliano Ferro glassworks, and then with Effetre International, though both ended without traumas. Silvano Tagliapietra, Lino's older brother, had married Maria Antonietta Ferro, affectionately known as Etta, from an ancient Murano glassmaking family, whose father Galliano Ferro had been a partner and founder of the important A.Ve.M. glassworks in 1932. Silvano joined the firm with a position in the workshop, but then quickly took on a top level management position. When his father-in-law left the old company in 1955 to set up the Galliano Ferro glassworks, Silvano went with him to take charge of management and especially the sales office. The new company, which now specialises in the production of chandeliers, at the time produced a vast range of products, including table services and decorative vases in traditional and modern styles, the latter designed by Giorgio Ferro, Etta's brother. In the same year, Lino left the Archimede Seguso glassworks and decided to join the Galliano Ferro glassworks, making one of the most fortunate choices of his career. He became the *servente* to the master Giovanni Ferro, called 'Nane Catari' (the same surnames have been repeated for centuries on the island, so nicknames were often used) discovering his vocation for glass work and becoming aware of his natural talent for this work, thanks also to the helpfulness and teaching skills of the master Catari. He found himself working in a *piazza* specialising in the production of goblets in traditional style.

The goblet may be considered the symbol of Venetian glassmaking since the 15th century and, as such, the item that has been most frequently reproduced by the great masters in their paintings since the Renaissance. The Venetian goblet with which Bacchus drinks a toast in the painting by Caravaggio, for example, now in the Uffizi, is a genuine icon. All the techniques of Venetian tradition are summed up in the goblet, but even when it does not have complex decorative patterns and stands out rather because of its elegant simplicity, it requires uncommon skill, control of the material and a sense of proportion, involving the master's hand and eye. Similar considerations are expressed by the American glass artist Dante Marioni, one of Lino's pupils, in his essay for the catalogue of the wonderful recent exhibition *Lino Tagliapietra, In Retrospect, A Modern Renaissance in Glass*, a travelling exhibition that visited some of the most important museums in the US.

In the positive climate of the Galliano Ferro glassworks, Lino Tagliapietra perfected his ability at shaping glass to such a point that in 1956 he was given the role of *maestrino*. The *maestrino* stands in for the *maestro* when necessary, and is basically a master on trial for a period during which his skills are appraised. The following year Lino became a *maestro*. Another positive choice made by Lino Tagliapietra in the 1950s was that of marrying Lino Ongaro, from a glassmaking dynasty dating back to the Renaissance, who has always accompanied him and supported his glassmaking ventures, such that his name is now as well known in the international glassmaking world as that of his famous wife. Specialisation in making goblets does not preclude other possibilities; on the contrary, it ensures an impeccable technical preparation that generally makes the master's move to other production sectors very easy. Not by chance was it Lino Tagliapietra who made the elegant, absolutely contemporary pieces - vases, goblets and candlesticks - designed by Giorgio Ferri in 1960 and 1962 and presented at the Venice Biennale in those years. In the 1960s Lino began conceiving the form of the *Saturno*, which he has developed in various forms and dimensions, perfecting its production methods over the years.

In 1966 Lino Tagliapietra left the Galliano Ferro glassworks due to tensions within the company and accepted an offer from the Venini glassworks to take up the *scagno* of the master for the production of goblets, and, occasionally, also vases. He spent 14 months at the Venini glassworks, a period he has defined as being very stressful because of the high level of competition between the masters. But among these, Checco Ongaro, Lino's brother-in-law, and Mario Tosi, called 'Mario Grasso', the main associate of the Finn Tapio Wirkkala, stood out for their human kindness and their extraordinary skill in the most complex processes. Lino still recognises his experience at Venini as beneficial because he had to come to grips with new ways of working the glass (in Murano there are various 'currents of thought' and various ways of obtaining a similar result) and a refinement of design unique in Murano. His relations with Ludovico Diaz de Santillana, director and artistic director of the Venini glassworks, were excellent, such that Diaz de Santillana himself was to subsequently compliment him on some of his glass collections.

The experience at Venini was useful, but its rapid negative conclusion may now be seen as a positive event in Lino Tagliapietra's career. From the time of its foundation in 1921, the Venini glassworks has maintained a rigorous distinction between roles, which has always been the irrefutable precondition of its production. The design stage is entrusted to internal designers and others called on from time to time, while the masters, some very highly qualified, have always played an exclusively production role, making some personal contribution but only within the limits of the designer's intentions. Certainly a skilled and open-minded master like Arturo Biasutto, called 'Boboli', in the company from 1925 to the 1950s, was always willing to look for completely new, previously untried approaches in order to achieve the result called for in the design, so at times the finished work could to some extent be credited to him. The same can be said of those masters who tried out new models in close contact with a designer inclined to give precise form to vague initial ideas in the course of creating the prototype. But no greater space was allowed to the master's personality and no Venini models are known to have been designed and signed by a master. So within this organisation Lino Tagliapietra would not have been able to pursue the ideas he was developing. This became possible when, after leaving Venini, he was taken on by the La Murrina glassworks in 1968, the same year the new company was founded.

La Murrina was set up by various members of the Moretti family, then owners of the big glass industry Ulderico Moretti & C., and the designer Gianmaria Potenza in the premises of the defunct Melloni & Moretti glassworks, owned by the same family. The artistic director was Gianmaria Potenza, but some models were designed by other associates such as Pietro Pelzel, Alessandro Lenarda and Bruno Teardo. The name of the new company came from the decorative *leitmotiv* of most of the collections: ranges of small, applied murrines or big murrines expanded by blowing in the middle of the piece. As first master Lino made the prototypes and the more demanding pieces among the decorative objects, table services and lighting glass. He gradually also devoted himself to designing objects and lamps, including the enduringly successful *Bovolo*, *Elmo*, *Formichiere* and *Varigola* table lamps. He also developed the *Saturno*, a slightly modified version of which was presented with Gianmaria Potenza's signature at the 1968 Venice Biennale. La Murrina was a company taking off, small and without any established rules, so in this environment marked by informal and friendly relations, the master found room to develop his creativity. In the last year of his stay at La Murrina, 1976, he took part in the First Course for Artists at the Scuola Internazionale del Vetro, an association of glass enthusiasts set up in 1975 with the aim of encouraging the renewal of Murano glassmaking. It organised the course to bring together master glassmakers and Italian and foreign artists unfamiliar with the world of glass. Each master worked with several artists and vice versa, to make experimental pieces at kilns made available by various Murano companies. Three courses were held in all: in 1976, 1978 and 1981. Among the most interesting works made by Lino Tagliapietra are those that arose out of his collaboration with the Paduan Emilio Baracco and the Slovenian Luigi Spacal in 1976, and especially those developed on the designs of Andries Dirk Copier in 1981. Andries Dirk Copier, the renowned designer who was active from the 1920s in Leerdam, Holland, came to Murano on the occasion of his 80th birthday to satisfy a long held desire to experience working in a Murano glassworks. The easiest way to gratify the grand old man of Dutch glassmaking was to add his name to the list of artists chosen for the Third Course for Artists held by the Scuola Internazionale del Vetro. On that occasion, Copier also worked with masters Mario 'Grasso' and Checco Ongaro from the Venini glassworks, but it was with Tagliapietra that he established a profound understanding that was destined to last, such that the two repeated the experience the same year and several other times until 1990. Apart from the high quality and innovation of the pieces made, this association was decidedly instructive for Lino, who was stimulated towards greater freedom in shaping the glass in search of a new

freshness of style, at times to the detriment of absolute regularity of form and decoration, in the light of an ideal of *sprezzatura*.

The resignation of the master, now also qualified as a designer, from La Murrina was not due to any lack of satisfaction with his position, but to the desire to embark on a new venture. He was offered the artistic and technical direction, along with the position of first master, at Effetre International, a new, small glassworks focusing on the production of decorative objects and lighting glass using traditional Murano techniques. It was backed by the larger Effetre, concentrating on semi-industrial production, and a third automated firm operating in Resana, in rural Veneto. The three 'Effe' (Fs) referred to the three Ferro brothers Guido, Ivano and Mario, each directing one of the companies. Mario, Lino's brother-in-law, was in charge of Effetre International, which proved to be a hothouse of new ideas. The everyday production was always of a high quality, but the one-off experimental pieces - made outside working hours - were quite exceptional. The standard items - the small series typical of Murano - and the one-off pieces were often marked by an unusual approach to the filigree technique, beyond the bounds of tradition, but with respect for the basic methods. There was an equally frequent use of *incalmo*, not only the usual horizontal *incalmo*, but also vertical, obtained by moving the axis of the blown piece during shaping. In this period Tagliapietra also began adding cold operations between two stages of hot working. He was to continue in this vein in the decades to come. A close examination of the works from this period, and the more recent ones, reveals the historical roots of some of the technical solutions he adopted, though they are not easy to recognise because so freely interpreted. In reality he is moved by a profound interest in the ancient, be it represented by an archaeological piece or a Renaissance one. But although the reproduction of traditional models was fundamental to his training, as it is to his teaching work, imitation is not even a consideration in his work. In the hours dedicated to experimentation at Effetre International, Lino was often accompanied at the kiln by Marina Angelin, a psychologist with no professional experience in either design or glassmaking techniques, but who has a marked sense of colour. It is difficult to appreciate the real extent of her influence on Lino Tagliapietra, now mature both as master and designer. It was probably her lack of glassmaking experience that led the young Marina to sketch out her models, so unorthodox that they would normally have been rejected by a glassmaker as being too difficult to translate into glass. But Lino felt stimulated to go beyond the canonical work methods, to adopt unusual chromatic combinations and to ignore the prevailing trends in glass design. His relations with American Studio Glass, which began in those years, were a similar stimulus for him. Having gone to Seattle for the first time to teach at the Pilchuck glass school in 1979 - as is well known - in place of his brother-in-law Checco Ongaro, he found himself in contact with emerging young artists who had none of the basic techniques ensured by ancient traditions, but who were also free of the conditioning that accompanies such traditions. They were incapable at the time of correctly working out a piece in glass, but full of enthusiasm and convinced that glass could be a valid expressive medium for their art. Far from Murano, Lino also became aware of his own resources. Since then he has taught continuously in various European countries and overseas, instructing numerous young glassmakers but also receiving much in return.

In 1989 he ended his association with Effetre International, which shortly after ceased trading independently of Effetre. Lino continued working as an independent artist, working in glassworks and glass studios in Murano and Seattle and devoting himself to the creation of one-off pieces sold in prestigious galleries and sought after by collectors and museum curators. Between 1991 and 1993, however, he had a very special working relationship with the EOS glassworks, run by the Venini family. Anna Venini and her husband Ludovico Diaz de Santillana had been bought out by the partners of their historic company in 1985. They had then set up EOS to design and market glass collections made in various glassworks. When Ludovico died, Anna Venini and her sons and daughters began the direct production of their collections in their own glassworks in Murano, with Laura de Santillana as artistic director. At EOS Lino agreed to a casual work commitment compatible with his obligations abroad, restricted to prototypes and the pieces of more complicated production. At the same time he had the use of a perfect base for making his own works. In 1998 he then opened his own glass studio with a small but perfectly equipped kiln in Murano, so part of his work is still done here. He restricts the making of large pieces, however, to the American studios, where he has qualified assistants on hand. Furthermore, his uncommon skill and ability to adapt have allowed him to create constantly differing works anywhere, compatible with the glass materials available, whether it be the glass made by CIRVA in Marseilles or the extremely pure lead crystal of the Steuben glassworks in Corning.

Making a critical reading of the overall development of Lino Tagliapietra's work is a fairly complex operation. This is because of the numerous experiences and cultural interests that have converged over the years to give form to his artistic vision, though this is in any case coherent, highly personal and always recognisable in the variety of its expressions. Fortified by a systematically structured technical training, he has always been open to other ideas, translating these into the glass language and harmoniously merging them in his works. The ideas are mainly derived from the history of art and the history of glass art, which an Italian, and especially a Venetian who works in the visual arts, can not easily avoid. Tagliapietra has always lived in a country - Italy - and a city - Venice - that boast a more than millennial history of art whose traces are evident everywhere. It has always been impossible for contemporary artists, even those who are part of avant-garde movements, to ignore these. Such has always been the case in the world of paint-

Lino sitting in the *scagno* at the designer Willem Heensen's De Oude Horn studio in Acquoy (Leerdam) with Adries Dirk Copier, 1990

Lino prepares his tools seated in the *scagno* in Dale Chihuly's Van de Kamp studio in Seattle, 1989

Lino making a butterfly for the *Borboleta* installation, Museum of Glass, Tacoma, 2009

ing, sculpture, architecture and of glass art. Tapio Wirkkala, for example, was a mature, established artist when he came to Venice in 1965 to work with Venini, but he realised - and it was he who said so - that he had to reckon with a city that is a genuine cultural melting pot with an ancient glassmaking tradition. His Venetian designs were to be very different from those for glass pieces made in Finland, inspired by the virgin nature of his country and his beloved Lapland, and arose rather out of a personal interpretation of historic Murano models. So while Tagliapietra is attentive to history, he has not restricted himself to correctly applying that which the old masters have handed down, nor to adopting the interpretations given to the ancient techniques by the grand glassmakers and masters of the 1930s and the fabulous fifties, but carries out his own research to then transform the idea from the ancient into something else.

Mention has already been made of his unconventional use of filigree and *incalmo* since the 1980s. But other experiments carried out in that same decade aimed at modernising past techniques must also be noted. They include the blowing of half-filigree pieces in ribbed moulds, which curve the straight canes, paying tribute to a technique in use at the end of the 16th century but bending it to give a new chromatic and plastic impact; the ice effect invented in the Renaissance, applied to two-colour glass sides resulting in branched clots of glass material; the very modern graphic play of decorations in split threads, that recall a Catalan 'façon de Venise' technique, also documented in the cabinets of the Murano Glass Museum.

The best examples of 20th-century glass work have also aroused the interest of Lino Tagliapietra, who has drawn his own inspiration from them, radically altering them. For example the *tessuto* bands of his recent *Provenza* vases (1999-2000), which seem covered by vibrant material brushstrokes in oils, are a long way from the accurate 'millerighe' *Tessuti* designed by Carlo Scarpa for Venini in 1938-1940. The question of the *battuto* conceived by Carlo Scarpa in 1940 and the related process of *inciso* becomes more complicated because the genesis of the technique itself is complicated. *Battuto* consists of making close circular and oval incisions over the entire surface of the glass wall. It is a typically Venetian wheel engraving technique that dulls the brilliance of the glass surface, giving it a tactile quality. The same quality is obtained by *inciso*, made with close, short, thin, linear incisions. But it is difficult to believe, as Helmut Ricke proposes in the catalogue for the *Lino Tagliapietra. In Retrospect* exhibition, that Carlo Scarpa was inspired to produce his *battuto* by the ground finishes of vases by Emile Gallé and Daum Frères, given the Venetian architect's tastes and the difficulty he would have had in examining French Art Nouveau glass in Venice in the 1930s. A technique similar to *battuto* can be seen on some precious Roman glasswork from the 1st century, of which some examples are now on show in the Murano Glass Museum, but they weren't there in the 1940s. This Roman technique was in turn inherited from the Sassanid and Islamic glassmakers of what is now Iran, however, and some examples of this have been visible since time immemorial in the Tesoro at St Mark's basilica in Venice. It was quite probably the latter that inspired Carlo Scarpa. In the early 1990s, when Scarpa's glass work was being reappraised, Murano rediscovered *battuto* and so did Lino Tagliapietra, who used it to advantage to create very large blown sculptural forms. But it was only some years later that he introduced *inciso* to his works, in an entirely personal version. In the past this process was applied to monochrome finished surfaces, but Lino Tagliapietra used it to give an entirely unexpected effect. The incisions, if applied to filigree or *tessuto* sides, upset and interrupt the lie of the glass canes, creating extremely refined irregular wefts.

Lino Tagliapietra is particularly fascinated by archaeological glass and his recent studies of the Roman glass collection in Altino have also borne fruit. The latest *Fuji* and *Osaka* collections conceal details inspired by the glass finds from the Roman city of Altino in their murrine fabrics, details that only an archaeologist could recognise, given the extreme modernity of the works. The *Avventura* installation of 2011 is also influenced by this study experience. An analysis of the historical sources in Lino Tagliapietra's work could continue infinitely, but then again, that of painting works by old masters and of ancient and modern sculpture also now calls for a detailed study of their stylistic and iconographic sources. The thing that makes Tagliapietra's work unique though is the impact American Studio Glass and his time in America have had on his work. The audacity of American artists has stimulated his own audacity; his familiarity with that country has driven him to attempt sizes unusual in Murano and unexpected and courageous colour combinations. Since 1996 he has also conceived big installations in highly coloured, blown glass, against the tendency in Murano to produce these only in pure crystal, a material in some ways similar to natural stone. Lino Tagliapietra knows how to look and above all to see. He is capable of appreciating the beauty of native American art, and some of his collections, the *Hopi* and the *Makah*, for example, were inspired by the tribes of those names; the former by the shapes of their ceramics, the latter by the weave of their baskets. It was for this ability of his to synthesise two worlds, along with his talent for teaching American glass artists that the museum of Tacoma in Washington state organised a vast retrospective exhibition on him in 2009, which then travelled to other important museums in the US. So it is fitting that Venice should also pay him tribute.

Maestro Lino

Tina Oldknow

*Glass is a wonderful material. Why? Because the glass is alive.
Even when it is cool, it is still moving. It is connected with fire,
it is connected with water, it is so natural. Glass is my life.–*

Lino Tagliapietra[1]

Lino working with Dale Chihuly on
a piece for the Venetians series,
Benjamin Moore studio, Seattle,
1989

If, as the American historian and philospher Will Durant wrote, 'education is the transmission of culture,' then Lino Tagliapietra is the reigning ambassador of Venetian glass. Venetian glassforming techniques are not only a style, they constitute a vibrant and unique craft language. And in the teaching of that language–a Muranese dialect–culture is transmitted and transformed.

The centuries-long and continuous history of the migration of Venetian glassworkers and glassforming techniques, from Murano to locations throughout Europe and the British Isles, is well known.[2] In the 20th century, however, something shifted: foreigners, many of them, came *to* Murano. Ten years ago, I was having a spirited conversation with Anna Venini, who observed that Venini was not only a factory, it was a culture and a school. This point of view impressed me. It is true that by 1937, with the arrival of the Swedish designer Tyra Lundgren at Venini, circumstances had changed. Lundgren was the first outsider to design for Paolo Venini, and the first woman to design on Murano. Her designs for Venini gave the company entrée into new markets in Scandinavia. This was the beginning of Venini's international retail presence that, along with those of other Muranese glass companies, would become well established by mid-century.

The 1950s and 1960s saw all kinds of artists coming to Murano, and not only to Venini. There was the little-known Texan sculptor, Robert Willson, who came to make his work with the master Alfredo Barbini, and of course the elite coterie of international art stars who circled around Peggy Guggenheim, whom she sent to her friend Egidio Costantini at the Fucina degli Angeli. Then, in 1968, Dale Chihuly arrived in the lagoon with his Super-8 video camera. When he stepped off the *vaporetto*, that was the moment American studio glass began to transform. Lino Tagliapietra was the means by which that process was completed. 'Lino's influence, and therefore Murano's, reshaped international glass,' writes contemporary glass critic and curator Susanne Frantz. 'If not for his teaching, the achievement of studio glass would have unfolded more slowly and surely at a different level and in a different form. ... How often does an artist accomplish something specific and concrete that opens new possibilities exceeding his or her own work and, as a result, affects the course of art history? Without hyperbole, that is the truth about Lino Tagliapietra and his influence on the history of blown glass.'[3]

The Old World: Murano

[Lino] gradually internalized a cultural universe during his extended apprenticeship. It was this process that enabled him to become a great technical master and, later, to redevelop his exceptional craft into art.–

Giovanni Sarpellon[4]

Lino Tagliapietra is an artist and glassblower who is one of a select few to achieve international recognition and success. He shows his vessels, sculptures, and installations from New York to Sydney to London. He makes his work in Murano and Seattle, and he has a prodigious exhibition schedule. In spite of his fame, he is remarkably grounded, and he is not a diva, which in American slang means overly tempermental and demanding. Somehow, he finds time to teach occasionally, through demos and master classes at colleges, art schools, and glass programs. He is justly revered as a great maestro and as an exceptional teacher by studio glass artists all over the world, but he is especially admired in the United States. He has brought his love of glass and his love of Murano to American artists, because you don't get Lino without Murano.

A couple of weeks ago, I heard an interview on the radio with the French master chef and international celebrity Jacques Pepin. He spoke about his apprenticeship in a country that is as possessive about its cooking as the Muranese are about their glassmaking. Pepin said that he learned by looking and doing, by osmosis, because the master chefs would never actually tell you how to do anything. You observed. Gradually, the chefs assigned Pepin increasing responsibilities. After some time working as a prep cook, he was told to make a stew, and he was terrified. But he discovered that, through his prep work, he knew what needed to be done. 'We learn differently today,' he said.

This interview gave me a tiny insight into what Lino's world must have been like during his apprenticeship with maestros such as Archimede Seguso and Giovanni Ferro. 'My education in glass was, of course, totally different than in America today,' Lino says. 'In Venice, you start doing very small things, whereas here people make larger pieces immediately. In Murano, we were young when we went into the glasshouses; we did not continue school. It was a different situation and different training than you get in the States, but I think it takes the same amount of time, one way or another, to make good work. [One] real difference is the culture, that knowledge of glass that is more in the minds of people in Murano. In Murano. . . it's like going to school and taking different subjects, everywhere there is glass. But, sometimes, if you know too much about glass, the glass itself will influence you. It is very important to develop original, fresh ideas.'[5] Lino adds that, 'the most valuable aspect of the traditional Murano education is that you have the chance to practice. All of the time!' Because there is so much glassworking on Murano, he explains, you have a

unique opportunity of seeing many different kinds of glass, many different ways of making it, and many new techniques, but it is up to you to figure out what the best way to make something might be.[6]

In 1978, the American studio glassblower Benjamin Moore spent several months at the Venini glassworks on Murano. As a result of his experience there, he recognized the importance of bringing Venetian masters to teach in the United States. Inspired by Dale Chihuly's stay on Murano in 1968, artists such as Richard Marquis and Jamie Carpenter had also gone to Venini, returning with technical tips that were surprisingly rudimentary, like the benefits of using a marver (that was big news, for young American artists, circa 1970).

Moore was the education coordinator at Pilchuck Glass School, in Washington, and although he had learned much about glassblowing during his time at Venini, he realized that his second-hand information had its limits. With the help of Chihuly, the school's founder and artistic director, Moore invited the master Franceso 'Checco' Ongaro, who he had met at Venini. Ongaro is a master with an unusually open mind, and throughout his career at Venini he was asked to work with visiting artists because he was personable and, most importantly, he enjoyed the challenge.

Ongaro was not the first to demonstrate to and teach Americans, however. Susanne Frantz explains that Italians were among the many European immigrants who found work in the American glass industry in the 19th and 20th centuries. While they were not all *maestri*, some trained glassmakers included Alessandro Moretti (1922-1998) and his brother Roberto Moretti (1930-1986), who began working at the Pilgrim Glass factory in Huntington, West Virgnia.[7] Yvonne Moretti, the daughter of Alessandro, says that her father was working in South Africa when he was hired, in 1956, by Pilgrim Glass to develop a new 'Italian Line.' His brother Roberto later came from Murano to the same factory in 1958. At the factory, there was an upstairs observation area where tourists could come to see the brothers work the glass.[8]

Harvey Littleton, of course, spent a month and half taking tourist tours on Murano in the late 1950s to find out if his idea of bringing hot glass to artists was even feasible. And, from the 1960s into the early 1980s, a procession of American artists had access to the entire Venini factory, thanks to the open-minded director Ludovico Diaz de Santillana. Marvin Lipofsky brought Gianni Toso to the California Bay Area to demo in 1976, Frantz writes, and Toso returned to teach in 1977 and again in 1983, and also made presentations to other American university art departments.[9]

Yet the experience with Ongaro at Pilchuck was very different, and Moore realized that the Pilchuck students needed more of this kind of instruction. Today, post-Lino, it is difficult to remember what early studio glassblowing was like. Fortunately, there is some video documentation. Just to mention one example, I found a grainy video in the Rakow Research Library of Dale Chihuly blowing glass with Jamie Carpenter in

1971 at the Haystack Mountain School of Crafts, in Maine.[10] The video documents Jamie and Dale making some of Chihuly's early, organically-shaped goblets. The stem was formed by pouring molten glass on the floor, and then tweezering up a hot mass and attaching it to the bottom of a blown cup, letting it stiffen, and then taking it to the annealer. All through the video, Chihuly is explaining the glassblowing process, and in comparison to how artists blow glass today, they look remarkably primitive. For one thing, they hardly reheat.[11]

'[American] artists who were working early on in the movement were trying to take glass out of the decorative arts… they wanted people to break barriers and to approach and use the material in a different way,' says Ben Moore. 'But everything was so primitive, as far as how things were executed… Technique is very important… It's repetition, it's craft, to build your vocabulary to be able to talk, and that was something that was severely lacking early on in the movement. The craft of making and wanting structure for me was very important. I was seeing all these lumpy, bumpy objects… To me, we needed more than that. That was a great starting point, but it had to go somewhere beyond in order for things to develop.'[12]

The New World: Pilchuck

As far as a Venetian glass master for Pilchuck '79 [goes], I have another dandy lined up. His name is Lino Tagliapietra… [He] speaks no English but will be great with the students. [He is] a very unique and rare Venetian glass master

Benjamin Moore[13]

After his summer at Pilchuck, Checco Ongaro decided not to return. However, he suggested to Ben Moore that his brother-in-law, Lino Tagliapietra, might be interested. I asked Lino once why he chose to come to the States. 'You know, I loved it,' Lino says. 'Even as a young kid, I liked the United States, and what it represented for the young kids in Murano at the time.' Lino had also worked in the factories for nearly 35 years. By the late 1980s, seven or eight years after his first trip to the States, he decided to retire and become independent. 'The factory became very uncomfortable, because the idea of blowing glass all day long, making lamps or making the production line all day long, I didn't like it so much, it became very hard to do it,' he says. 'I discovered the opportunity to have a change, and I took big steps, you know?'[14] Lino came to America to discover what there might be here for him and to teach others to work glass. In the process, he helped to pioneer a new industry—not for commerce, but for art.

Upon his arrival at Pilchuck in 1979, and into the 1980s, Lino had to make some adjustments. Although he was pleasantly surprised by the freedom and open attitude of the artists toward the material, he had to work with stiff glass of 'terrible' quality, with terrible benches and terrible tools. 'They were working the glass very cold, it was very odd, the glory hole was terrible,' Lino recalls. 'I tried to do the *reticello*, but the *pastorale* didn't heat... The artists had an incredible focus on what they were doing, but their techniques, they were very poor.'[15]

Although some of the artists teaching at Pilchuck had been to Italy, and others had seen demonstrations of Italian techniques, there was no substitute for seeing the processes performed by a master. 'For the first time there was someone who actually could make things perfectly and easily,' Richard Marquis recalls. 'Harvey Littleton's "technique is cheap" slogan sounded a little tiresome in the face of this guy who could blow on center. For some glassblowers, worlds started to change.'[16] Fritz Dreisbach 'was struck by the different ways that Lino tweezed and snipped the glass, and how he kept it very hot by repeated trips to the glory hole.'[17] Lino offered insights into everything from how to correctly gather glass onto a pipe to how to knock the finished vessel off of it. Norman Courtney recalls that 'Everybody realized that we had been doing it wrong.' Paul Marioni remembers that when Lino was blowing, someone would bring him a gather and he would say, 'What's this? Bring me something hot!'[18]

Lino did not coddle his students. He expected them to pay close attention. When asked about marvering the hot glass that first summer, Fritz Dreisbach remembers, 'Lino's response was, "You have to search to know."'[19] Dante Marioni realized 'how important it was to do just like Lino, to emulate his every move, whether I fully understood what I was doing or not. By absorbing his disciplined values, instead of taking an easier approach, one eventually begins to understand and "find the feeling" for the glass.'[20]

As American students absorbed what Lino had to offer, Lino also learned from them. At first taken aback by the casual attitudes of American glassblowing students, their freedom and lack of hesitation with hot glass made an impression. '[They were] quite strong... not for the technique, but for the energy,' Lino explains. 'I saw the potential in these people, the movement.'[21] He adds, 'The boldness was so new to me. On the one hand, it was a shock—the lack of a cultural base, the absence of traditions. But on the other hand, it was exhilarating—the lack of restraint in the process, the exciting results.'[22]

Lino was not the only European to teach at Pilchuck during the summer of 1979. The Swedish artist Ann Wolff arrived with her gaffer, Wilke Adolfson. British stained-glass artists Brian Clarke and Patrick Reyntiens showed up, along with the German artists Ludwig Shaffrath and Klaus Moje. Over the next couple of years, Lino was joined by Swedes Bertil Vallien and Ulrica Hydman-Vallien, German artist Erwin Eisch, and Czechs Stainslav Libenský and Jaroslava Brychtová. Like Lino, Moje and Vallien returned year after year, so there was an ongoing European influence.[23] Ben Moore remembers working with the students, who were

Lino working with Dante Marioni, his assistant, during a course at the Haystack Mountain School of Crafts, Deer Isle, Maine, 1994

Lino working watched by Richard Royal (left) and Benjamin Moore in the Van de Kamp studio of Dale Chihuly, who watches him from behind, 1988-89

'vibrant young artists who were so hungry. They were like sponges when these Europeans came in. The designers and artists from different countries, sharing their cultural differences and backgrounds, created a melting pot that was incredible.'[24]

Although Scandinavian- and Czech-style glassmaking was influential, the Venetians in general, and Lino in particular, played the most significant role in the development of contemporary American glass. For Americans, Lino opened a path onto centuries of craft knowledge. Learning Venetian glassblowing techniques enabled American studio glass artists to greatly expand their technical vocabularies, which, with the addition of new and experimental approaches, led to the artistic redefinition of the material.

'When Nane Ferro found out I was coming to the States to teach, he told me, "What you do is your business, but don't teach too much. Because what you have learned is not just yours. It is part of a tradition and it's not right that you give it to everybody,"' Lino remembers. 'I replied that I thought that everything we learn comes from somewhere or somebody else, knowledge does not belong to anyone. No one person brought technique to Murano. This is an important point because glassblowers must work together to develop their skills, to push themselves to do something different. What I like about the American studio glass movement is that people share everything. They want everyone to have all the information, yet no one has taken another's place. There is room for everyone.'[25]

In spite of having worked for decades in the factories of Murano, Lino fundamentally understood the nature of the passion for glass that the young American artists were experiencing. 'Glass requires a lot of technique,' Lino says. 'If you are limited in technique, it is quite difficult for you to have a new idea because all of your energy is focused on learning how to do it. You must have passion, curiosity, humility. But, you know, technique is never enough… You must be always ready for something else. I try every day to invent something, every single day… I also think, if you do not know what people did in the past, how is it possible to make new things?'[26]

Glass, Italian-American Style

[I have] a hand-tinted photograph attributed to Paolo Salviati,
taken at the turn of the century, of Buffalo Bill and Sitting Bull
in a gondola in the Venice lagoon. [And then I have] a photograph
of Lino Tagliapietra getting out of my 1934 Plymouth in the small
island town where I live. These two pictures represent what I think
are the two most important cultural transactions between Italy
and the United States... In my opinion, Lino has been the single most
positive and significant influence on young glassblowers in this country
and elsewhere. He has shared his skills, patience, and charisma freely...
Lino has always had the big picture in mind. Ancient traditions will
continue because of this man. We owe him so much, we all know that.–

Richard Marquis[27]

Looking back–50 years from now–on studio glass from the 1980s and 1990s, we might say that the widespread use of Muranese glassforming techniques by American artists created a renaissance in Venetian glass. And perhaps the Venetian impact on contemporary studio glass, especially in the United States, will be considered as another chapter in the long and complex history of the *façon de Venise*.

Venetian glassworking techniques have acted as a catalyst for international studio glass artists. Italian-style glassblowing has inspired artists to explore additional paths in glass, and it has flourished not only in the United States, but in such unexpected places as Australia. The studio glass artist's peripatetic lifestyle–traveling and demonstrating at studios and conferences around the globe–has resulted in the dissemination of an incredible wealth of glassmaking knowledge.

Lino's exceptional talent, knowledge, and teaching ability have given direction to the careers of many artists today who work in glass throughout the world. Artists use a Venetian glass vocabulary to make vessels and sculpture that would never, ever be produced on Murano, and the dissemination of this remarkably creative and versatile craft language may be Lino's most important legacy. Glass is a technically demanding medium, and Venetian glassworking techniques are important tools with which contemporary artists realize their ideas. The best artists today do not copy Italian glass. Instead, they reinterpret and extend its distinctive approach to form and decoration.

As much as Lino gave to American artists, however, he took from American art and culture for his own use. In 1988, he made the difficult decision to change his artistic focus from design to unique work, a step that initiated years of self-examination. This change was inspired, in no small part, by Lino's work with artists such as Dale Chihuly. 'My ideas about Venetian glass gradually shifted, through a long and difficult process, to become focused on artistic expression,' Lino observes. 'When you make a unique object, it takes a totally different energy. The shape, the technique, the root of the piece might be more or less the same, but you have to completely change your approach to making the object.'[28] Lino may have been influenced by the attitudes of American artists, but he was especially impressed by American art. An admirer of indigenous and modern American art, Lino finds inspiration in native American textiles, the paintings of Jackson Pollock, and the architecture and design of Frank Lloyd Wright. 'What intrigues me even more than the energy in these works is the division of the space,' Lino says. 'The division of space, the broken wall, the division where it is possible to be shocked. This is what I am always looking at... I also admire the art of the native Americans. In this art, I find a very strong expression of American culture, and I think it is the native contribution to the culture that makes America so unique.'[29]

Not only did Lino look at American art and culture, he internalized it. How, for example, did he think to translate an American pop icon, such as Batman, into his repertoire of Italian forms? Or, how has he interpreted native American textiles to influence his bold palette? Lino learned how to be a designer and maker in Murano, but he learned how to be an artist in America. Technical virtuosity aside, his pieces also have a strong spiritual component: they have soul. Lino has not been afraid to experiment, he has not been afraid to make mistakes and, as is often the case, he has benefited immensely from the risks he has taken with his art.

[1] Robin Lehman, *Glass Masters at Work: Lino Tagliapietra*, Corning, NY: The Studio of The Corning Museum of Glass, 2008, color DVD, 59 min. The title of this essay is taken from Richard Marquis's article in *American Craft* cited below: it is the respectful, yet friendly, way Lino is addressed by American artists.

[2] See, for example, the recent publication by Jutta-Annette Page (ed.), *Beyond Venice: Glass in Venetian Style, 1500-1750*, New York: Hudson Hills Press, 2004.

[3] Susanne K. Frantz, *Lino Tagliapietra in Retrospect: A Modern Renaissance in Italian Glass*, Tacoma, WA: Museum of Glass, 2008, p. 25.

[4] Giovanni Sarpellon, *Lino Tagliapietra*, Venice: Arsenale Editrice, 1994, p. 18. Lino claims that his training took more time than some of his peers because he was not 'a natural.' Richard Marquis, 'Maestro Lino,' *American Craft*, December, 1997/January, 1998, p. 42.

[5] Tina Oldknow, 'Conversation with Lino Tagliapietra,' *Glass Art Society Journal*, Seattle: Glass Art Society, 1997, p. 12-13.

[6] Tina Oldknow, 'Conversazione con Lino Tagliapietra / Conversation with Lino Tagliapietra.' *Vetro*, April - June, 1999 (Anno 2, No. 3), Centro Studio Vetro, Murano, Italy, p. 31.

[7] Frantz, p. 28-29, footnote 27.

[8] Yvonne Moretti, email correspondence, October, 2010.

[9] Frantz, p. 28-29, footnote 27.

[10] Bob Hanson, Dale Chihuly, and Jamie Carpenter, 'Glass Blowing', New York: American Craft Council, 1971, b/w video, 13 min.

[11] The video documentation by Seattle artist Buster Simpson of the early years at Pilchuck Glass School is another important resource. With the support of The Rakow Research Library at The Corning Museum of Glass, Pilchuck recently converted the deteriorating videos into a more stable DVD format.

[12] Tina Oldknow, 'Meet the Artists: Debora Moore and Benjamin Moore,' The Corning Museum of Glass podcast, November 30, 2007.

[13] Letter from Ben Moore to Tom Bosworth, February, 1979. Tina Oldknow, *Pilchuck: A Glass School*, Seattle: Pilchuck Glass School in association with the University of Washington Press, 1996, p. 160.

[14] Tina Oldknow, 'Meet the Artist: Lino Tagliapietra,' The Corning Museum of Glass podcast, May 15, 2007.

[15] Ibid.

[16] Marquis, p. 42.

[17] Frantz, p. 15.

[18] Oldknow, *Pilchuck*, p. 163-164.

[19] Frantz, p. 15.

[20] Dante Marioni in Frantz, p. 40.

[21] Tina Oldknow, 'Meet the Artist: Lino Tagliapietra.'

[22] Oldknow, *Pilchuck*, p. 163.

[23] Oldknow, *Pilchuck*, p. 276-277. Other Muranese maestros who came to Pilchuck in the 1980s were Pino Signoretto and Loredano and Dino Rosin. In the 25 years since, many accomplished Italian glassblowers and flameworkers have taught in the United States and in studios around the world.

[24] Tina Oldknow, 'Meet the Artists: Debora Moore and Benjamin Moore.'

[25] Oldknow, *Glass Art Society Journal*, p. 13.

[26] Lehman, *Glass Masters at Work: Lino Tagliapietra.*

[27] Richard Marquis, 'Lifetime Achievement Award Presentation to Lino Tagliapietra,' *Glass Art Society Journal*, Seattle: Glass Art Society, 1997, p. 8, 10.

[28] Tina Oldknow, *Vetro*, p. 24.

[29] Tina Oldknow, 'Interview with Lino Tagliapietra,' *Lino Tagliapietra at Bullseye Glass: Masterworks from Furnace and Kiln* (Portland, Oregon: Bullseye Glass Company), 1999, p. 12; Oldknow, *Glass Art Society Journal*, p. 14.

Catalogue of works

Goblet
1954
h 10 cm x ⌀ 10 cm
blown glass, applied stem
and foot
private collection

Vase
Vetreria Ferro Galliano
1956
h 23.5 cm x ⌀ 24 cm
twisted filigree blown glass
design Vinicio Vianello
production Lino Tagliapietra
signed double signature
of Vinicio Vianello
Compasso d'oro prize 1957
Maurizio Graziani collection,
Venice

Goblet in opalescent glass, goblet and candlestick in transparent glass
Vetreria Ferro Galliano
1960, 1962
opalescent goblet
h 19.5 cm x ⌀ 19.5 cm
blue goblet h 28 cm x ⌀ 10 cm
green candlestick
h 38 cm x ⌀ 10 cm
candlestick with red base
h 39 cm x ⌀ 9 cm
blown glass
Paola Ferro collection, Venice

Vases in transparent glass
Vetreria Ferro Galliano
1962
pink vase h 33.5 cm x w 10 cm
x d 7 cm
yellow vase h 32 cm x w 11 cm
x d 8 cm
blue vase h 38 cm x w 13 cm
x d 10 cm
blown glass, obtained by
constriction during manufacture
Paola Ferro collection, Venice

Saturno Cup
Vetreria La Murrina
1969
h 10 cm x ⌀ 37 cm
blown amethyst glass
private collection

Saturno Cup
Vetreria La Murrina
1968
h 5 cm x ⌀ 21 cm
blown opalescent glass
Sandro Pezzoli collection, Milan

Bowl and saucer
Vetreria La Murrina
1970
piattino h 3 cm x ⌀ 20 cm
ciotola h 8 cm x ⌀ 24.5 cm
blown amethyst glass
private collection

Formichiere (anteater)
Lamp-sculpture
Vetreria La Murrina
1973
h 30 cm x w 65 cm x d 17 cm
blown glass
private collection

Sculpture
Vetreria La Murrina
1976
sphere ⌀ 10 cm
cone h 15 cm x ⌀ 10 cm
cords 35 cm x h 18 cm x 5 cm
32 cm x h 18 cm x 10 cm
half-filigree blown glass
design Emilio Baracco
production Lino Tagliapietra
private collection

Cups
Vetreria Effetre International
1981
h 18 cm x ⌀ 31 cm
blown glass with vertical canes
and spiral thread
design Andries Dirk Copier
production Lino Tagliapietra
signed «Lino Tagliapietra F3I A.D.
Copier - 81 - 09 - 02»
h 27 cm x ⌀ 24 cm
blown glass with incalmo and
half-filigree
design Andries Dirk Copier
production Lino Tagliapietra
signed «Da Andries D. Copier a
Lino Tagliapietra maggio 1981»
private collection

Vase
Vetreria La Murrina
1976
h 25 cm x w 22 cm x d 13 cm
blown glass with glass powders,
canes and murrine
design Luigi Spacal
production Lino Tagliapietra
signed «Spacal + Talia 1976»
Massimo Nordio collection, Venice

Mogambo
Vetreria Effetre International
1982
vase h 33 cm x w 27 cm x d 13 cm
signed «Effetre International
Murano 1990 Lino Tagliapietra»,
bowl h 3.5 cm x w 19.5 cm x d
19 cm
signed «Effetre International
Murano 1990 Lino Tagliapietra»
Anna and Attilio Locci collection,
Novara

Piumette (Little Feathers)
1982
h 35 cm x w 24 cm
interrupted cane glass,
made at CIRVA, Marseilles
private collection

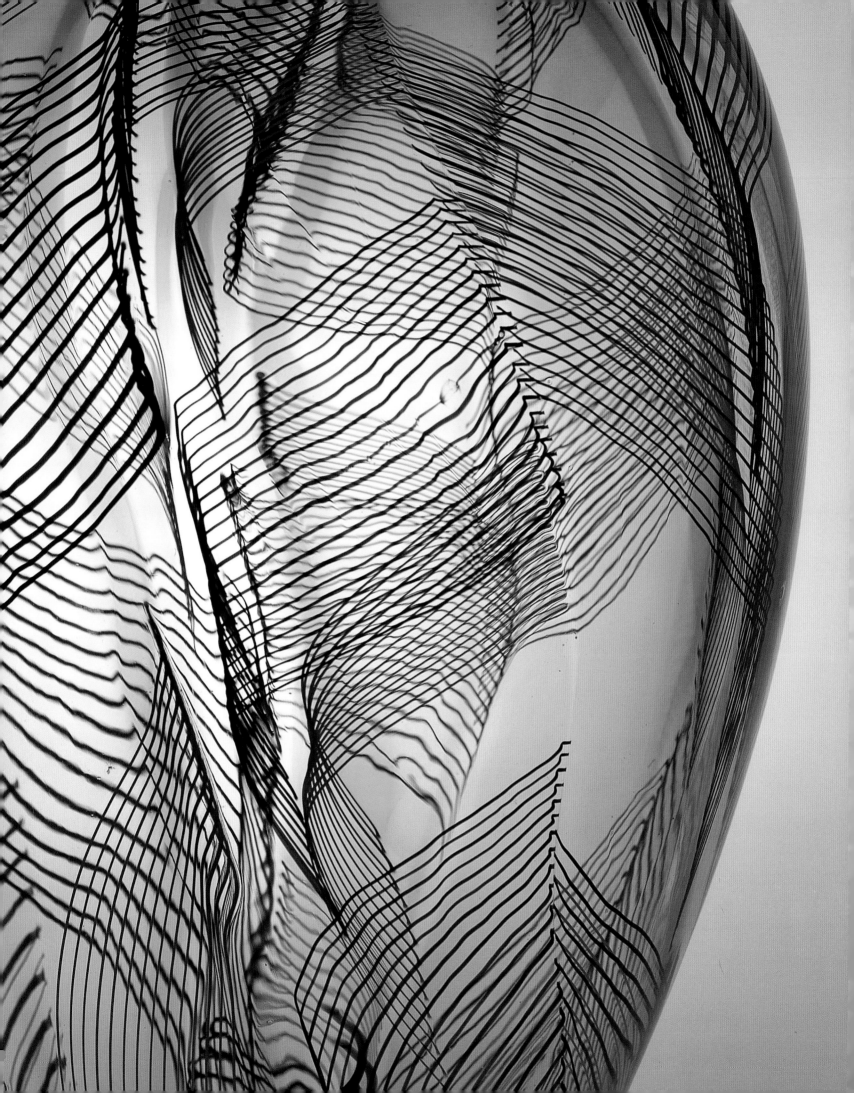

Square Eggs
Vetreria Effetre International
1984-1987
blown glass with applications of
canes and murrine
red h 26 cm x 12 cm
signed «Lino Tagliapietra Effetre
International Murano 1986»
black h 38 cm x 12 cm
signed «Lino Tagliapietra 1987
Murano»
private collection
Massimo Nordio collection, Venice

Eggs
Vetreria Effetre International
for the American company
Oggetti
1982-1983
blown glass with applications of
canes and murrine
white h 21 cm x ⌀ 16 cm
yellow h 16 cm x ⌀ 12 cm
red h 24 cm x ⌀ 17 cm
violet h 18 cm x ⌀ 14 cm
black h 24 cm x ⌀ 17 cm
grey h 11,5 cm x ⌀ 9,5 cm
private collection

Bowl
1985
h 7.5 cm x ⌀ 14 cm
grey and opaline half-filigree
glass, overlaid with opaline,
double turned
private collection

Vase
Vetreria Effetre International
1985
h 22 cm x ⌀ 29 cm
black and white half-filigree glass,
overlaid with black glass,
turned rim
private collection

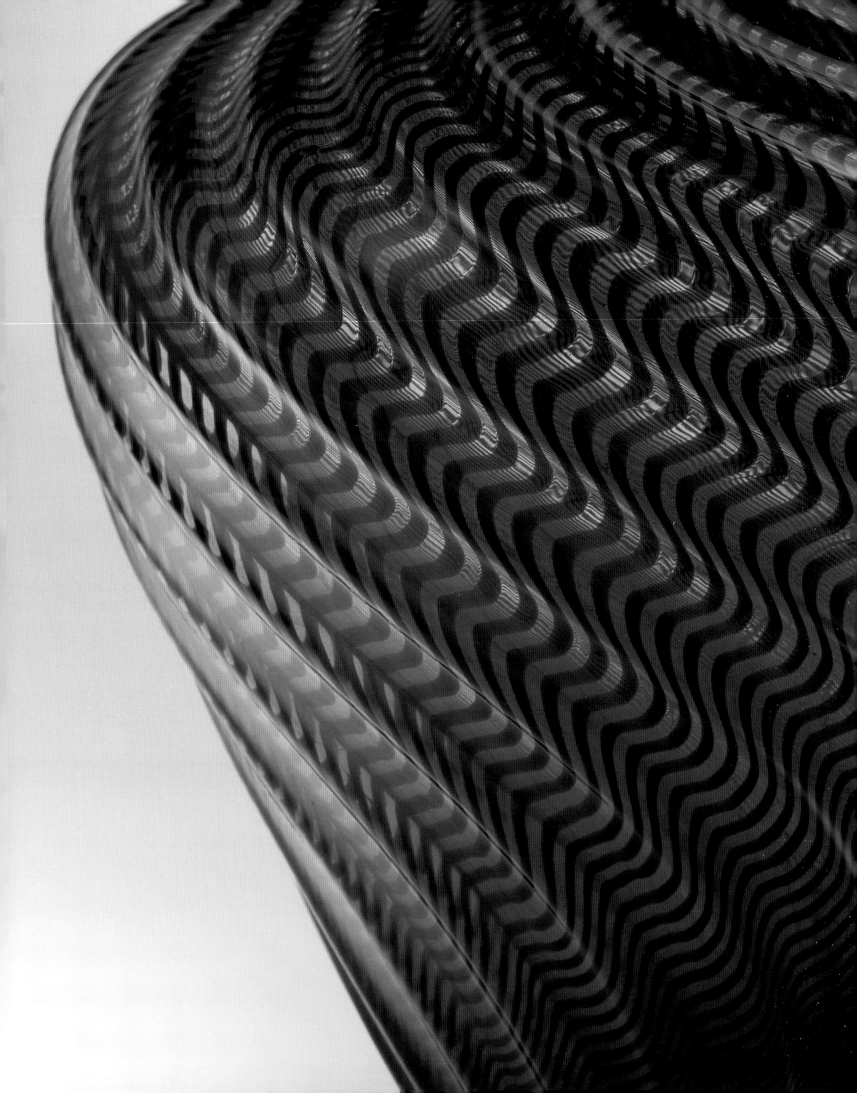

Vase
Vetreria Effetre International
1983
h 24 cm x ⌀ 22 cm
mould blown, half-filigree glass
private collection

**La donna in jeans
(The Woman in jeans)**
Vetreria Effetre International
1984
w 32 cm
h 29 cm
w 21 cm
blown cane glass, cold ground
overlaid hot with crystal
Sandro Pezzoli collection, Milan

Pueblo bowl and vase
Vetreria Effetre International
1985
bowl h 15 cm x ⌀ 25 cm
vase h 33 cm x ⌀ 21 cm
blown cane glass with spiral
thread
private collection

Rainbow
Vetreria Effetre International
1985
h 25 cm x ⌀ 25 cm
blown polychrome cane glass
in relief
signed «Lino Tagliapietra 1985»
private collection

Space city
1984
h 36 cm x ⌀ 21 cm
incalmo *Saturno* on glass stem
signed «Lino Tagliapietra Murano
84»
Massimo Nordio collection, Venice

Space needle
1985
h 31 cm x ⌀ 22 cm
triple incalmo blown glass
Massimo Nordio collection, Venice

Vase
c. 1986
h 23 cm x ⌀ 18 cm
blown half-filigree glass with
applications of crystal
Sandro Pezzoli collection, Milan

Cup
Vetreria Effetre International
c. 1987
h 15 cm x ⌀ 36 cm
blown glass with application of
solid cane glass sphere
prototype (never put into
production)
private collection

Tessuto (Fabric) Vases
Vetreria Effetre International /
Murano
1985
green vase: h 21 cm x w 29 cm
red vase: h 29 cm x w 22 cm
white vase: h 34 cm x w 20 cm
blown glass, overlapping canes,
ground
Sandro Pezzoli collection, Milan

Tessuto (Fabric) Vase
Vetreria Effetre International
1987
h 30 cm x w 29 cm x d 14 cm
glass in overlapping layers with
canes and spiral threads
signed «Lino Tagliapietra 1987»,
Massimo Nordio collection, Venice

Tessuto (Fabric) Vases
1988
h 39 cm x w 22 cm x d 12 cm
glass in overlapping layers with
canes and spiral threads, ground
signed «Lino Tagliapietra 1988
prova d'autore»
Massimo Nordio collection, Venice

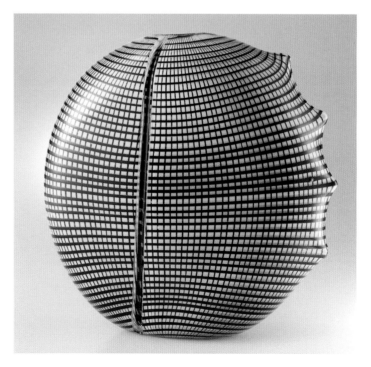

Vase
1987
h 30 cm x w 17 cm x d 13 cm
blown cane glass with broken
spirals
signed «Lino Tagliapietra 1987»
Massimo Nordio collection, Venice

Cobbled vase
1989
h 32 cm x ⌀ 15 cm
blown glass with polychrome
applications
signed «Lino Tagliapietra 1991»
private collection

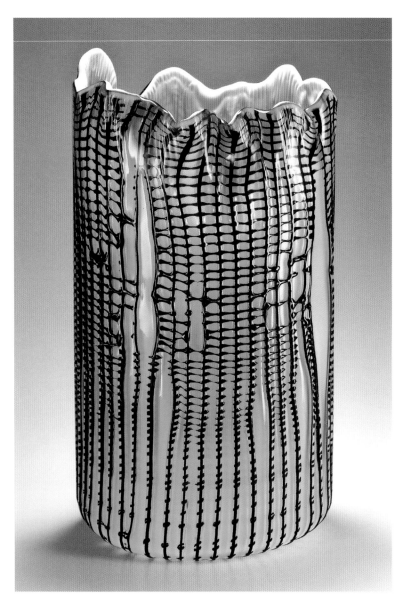

Black and Brown
1990
h 24 cm x ⌀ 24 cm
h 22 cm x ⌀ 24 cm
mould blown half-filigree glass,
ground
Sandro Pezzoli collection, Milan

Venetian
1988
h 60 cm x w 37 cm x d 35 cm
blown glass with applications of
shards and hot moulded ropes
design Dale Chihuly
production Lino Tagliapietra
private collection

**Notte del Redentore
(Night of the Redentore)**
1985
h 41 cm x w 14 cm x d 9 cm
blown glass with polychrome
bands and applied threads
signed «Lino Tagliapietra 1995»
private collection

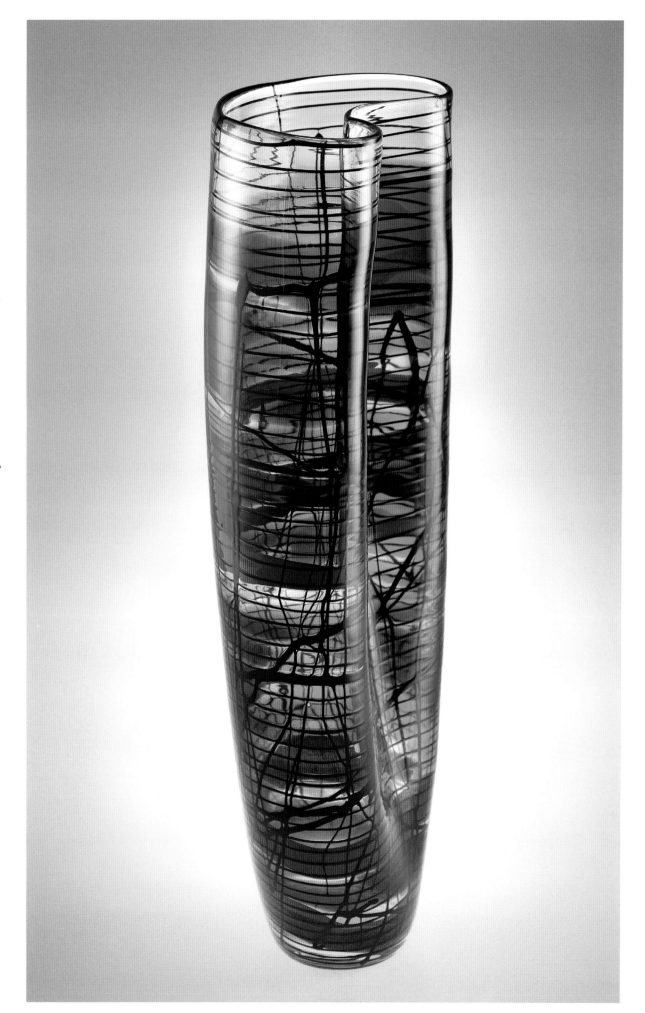

Miniature vases
1990
from left
h 8 cm x ⌀ 4.5 cm
h 15 cm x w 8 cm x d 4 cm
h 7 cm x ⌀ 4.5 cm
h 8 cm x ⌀ 4.5 cm
h 15.5 cm x w 5.5 cm x d 5 cm
h 8.5 cm x ⌀ 4 cm
h 14.5 cm x w 6 cm x d 3 cm
enamel painted blown glass
design and enamelling Dan Dailey
production Lino Tagliapietra
signed «DT 90»
private collection

Vase
c. 1990
h 62 cm x w 25 cm x d 22 cm
enamel painted blown glass
design and enamelling Dan Dailey
production Lino Tagliapietra
private collection

Vase
1991
h 27 cm x ⌀ 15 cm
blown glass with applications and
spiral thread
Liana and Mario De Antonellis
collection, Milan

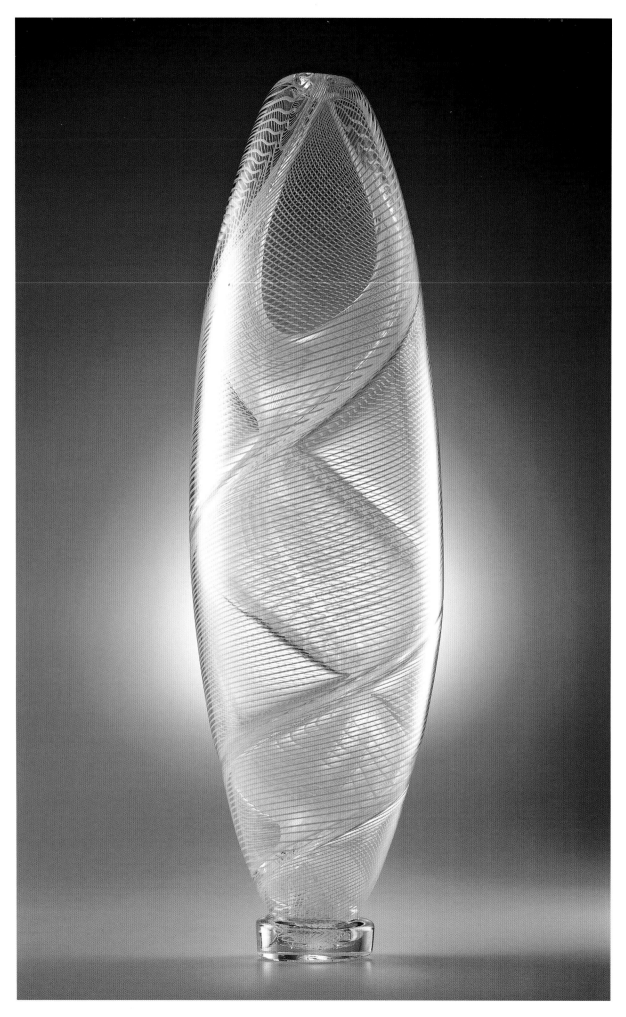

Spiral Vase
1992
h 40 cm x ⌀ 11 cm
half-filigree blown glass
with internal membrane
signed «Lino Tagliapietra 1992»
private collection

Spiral Goblets
1991-1993
from left: h 19 cm x ⌀ 9.5 cm
h 22 cm x ⌀ 8 cm
h 25 cm x ⌀ 7 cm
h 24 cm x ⌀ 8.5 cm
half-filigree blown glass
with internal membrane
private collection

Vase
1991
h 37 cm x w 22.5 cm
blown glass, applied powders,
overlaid
project Lino Tagliapietra, Alfred
De Credico, Toots Zynsky
Production Lino Tagliapietra
Sandro Pezzoli collection, Milan

**Notte del Redentore
(Night of the Redentore)**
1992
h 15 cm x ⌀ 14 cm
blown glass with polychrome
bands
and applied threads
signed «Lino Tagliapietra»
private collection

Saturno
1992
h 29 cm x ⌀ 9 cm
amethyst and green blown glass
signed Lino Tagliapietra
private collection

**Sasso di Marsiglia
(Marseilles Stone)**
1992
h 25.5 cm x ⌀ 25 cm
painted, sommerso, blown glass
with spiral thread
Sandro Pezzoli collection, Milan

**Sassi di Marsiglia
(Marseilles Stone)
series Plate**
1992
h 6 cm x w 50 cm x d 36 cm
blown glass painted and worked
hot
private collection

Vase
1993
h 40 cm x w 15 cm x d 12 cm
blown glass with twisted filigree
canes in dichroic glass
private collection

Relief Ribbon Vases
1994
violet vase h 29 cm x w 25 cm x
d 13 cm
green vase h 19 cm x ⌀ 20 cm
signed «Lino Tagliapietra 1994»
blown glass with twisted ribbons
applied in relief
private collection

River stone Vase
1996
h 36 cm x w 33 cm x d 13 cm
triple incalmo blown glass with
murrine band
artist's collection

Handkerchief
1996
h 24 cm x w 55 cm x d 34 cm
'fabric' blown glass
signed «Lino Tagliapietra 96»
artist's collection

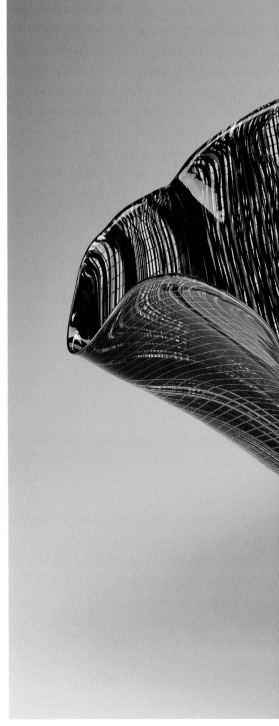

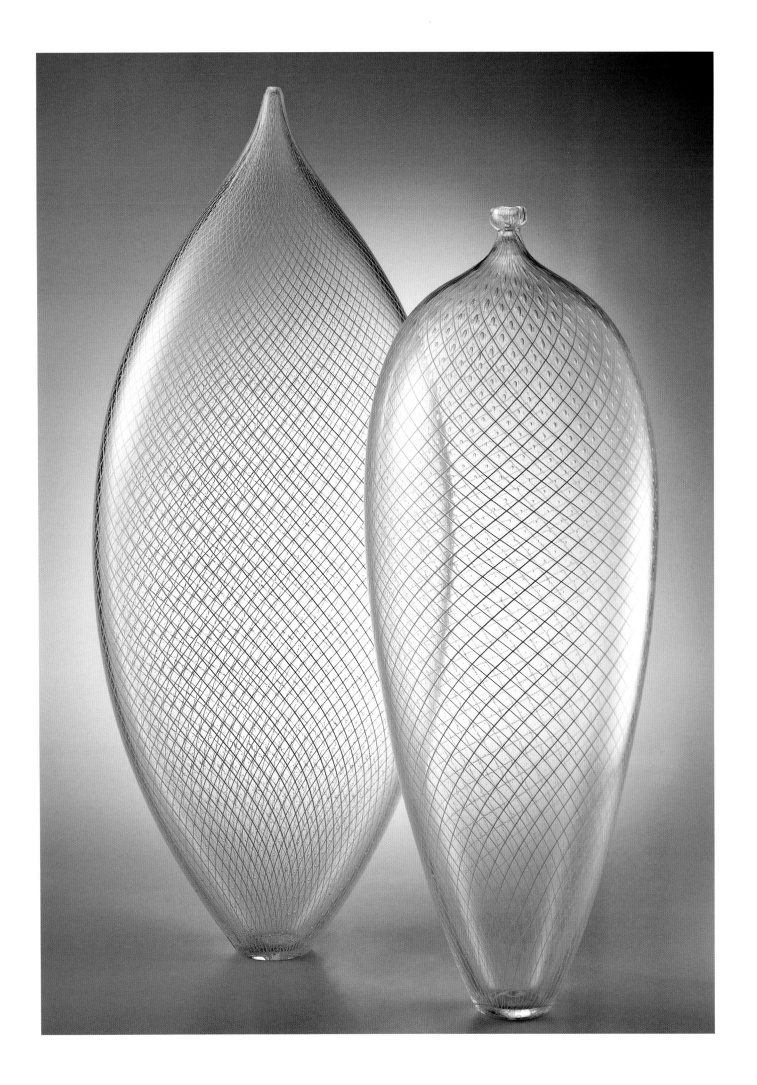

Vases
1996
h 59 cm x w 25 cm x d 10 cm
h 49 cm x ⌀ 18 cm
blown reticello filigree glass
the first signed «Lino Tagliapietra
1996»
artist's collection

Vase
1998
h 49 cm x ⌀ 13 cm
blown, ground and engraved
crystal
made at the Steuben glassworks
in Corning N.Y.
private collection

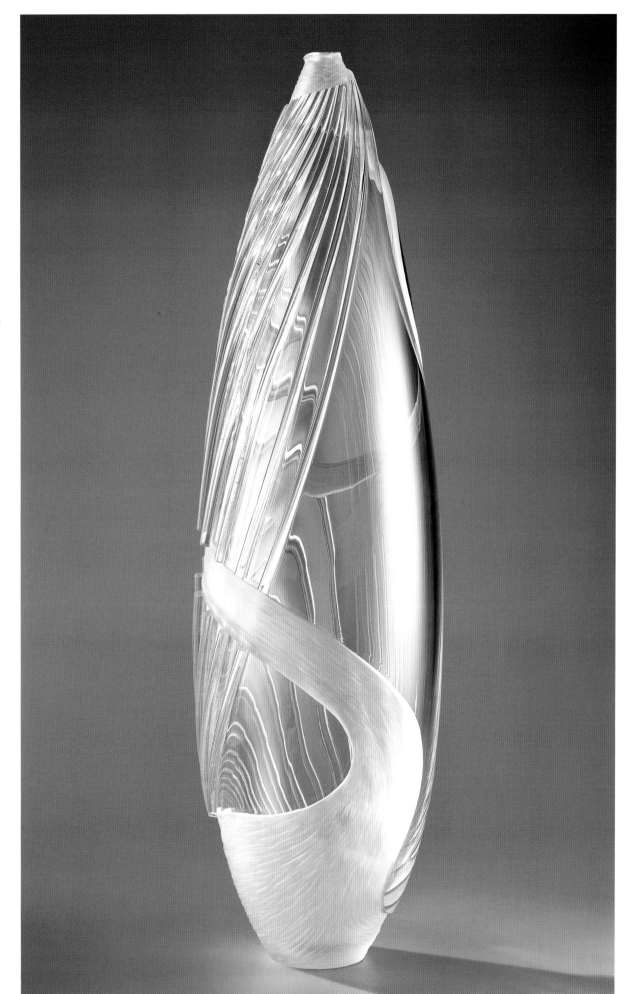

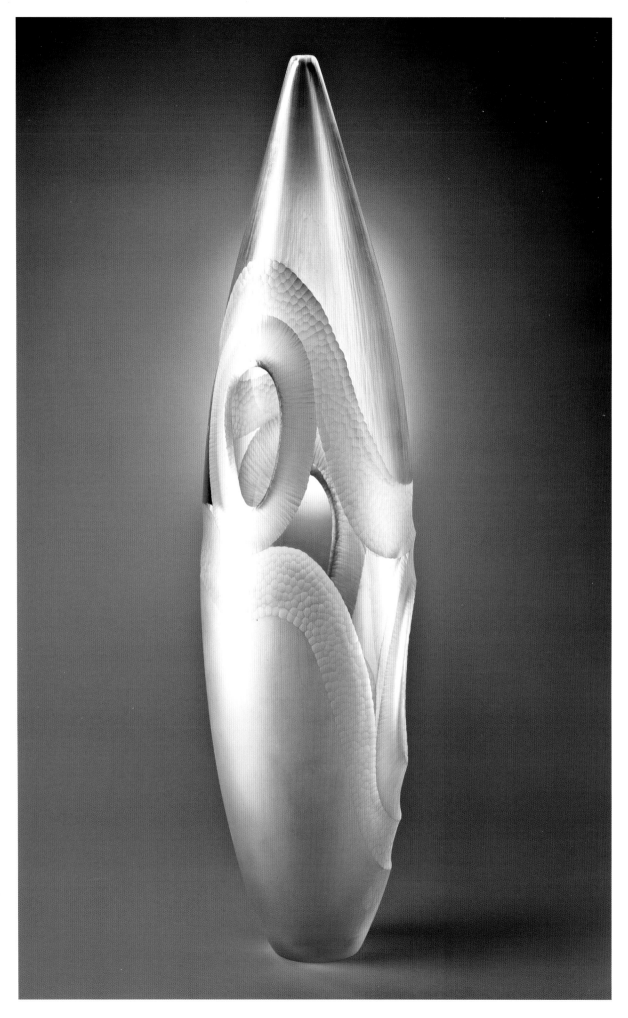

Vase
1998
h 60 cm x ⌀ 14 cm
blown crystal, ground, pierced
and battuto
made at the Steuben glassworks
in Corning N.Y.
private collection

Tholtico
1998
h 50 cm x ⌀ 23 cm
blown glass, overlaid and cameo
engraved
signed «Lino Tagliapietra 1998»
artist's collection

Vase
1998
h 19 cm x ⌀ 14 cm
engraved, blown glass
private collection

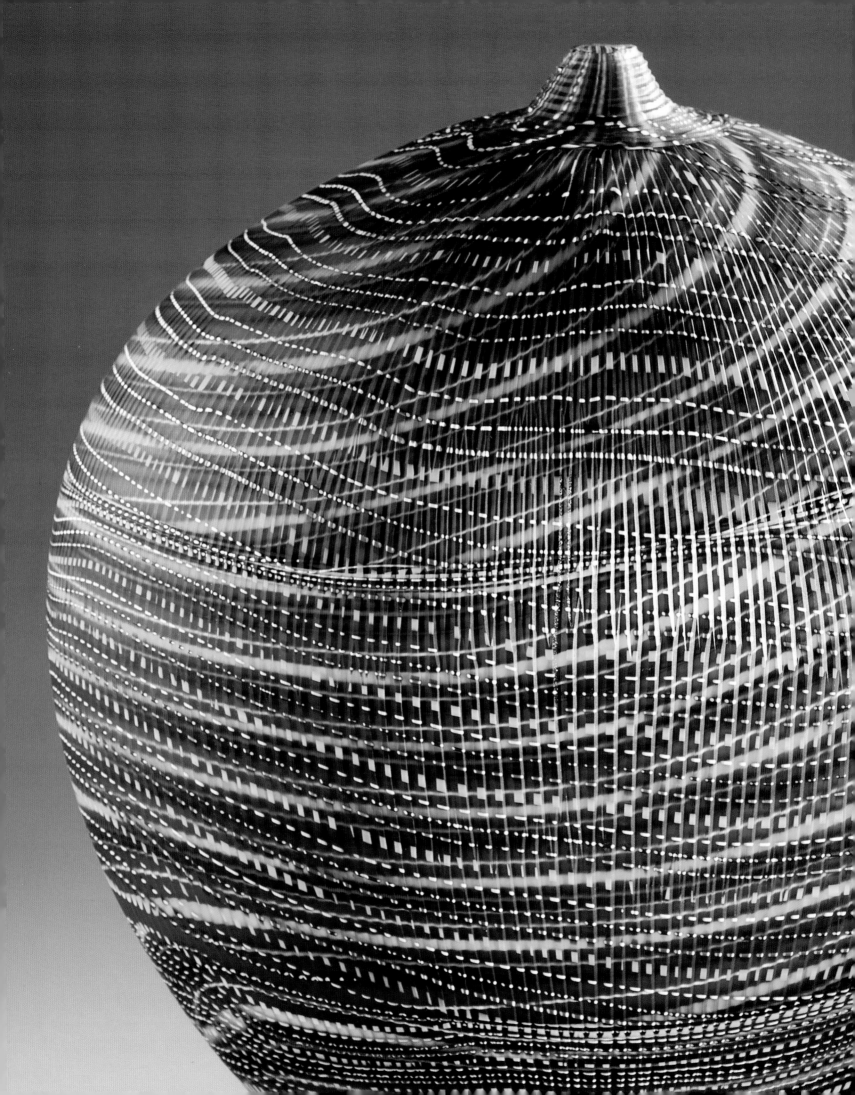

Fado
1998
h 30 cm x w 27 cm x d 22 cm
blown multilayered cane glass
with spiral threads
artist's collection

Madras
1999
h 42.5 cm x w 31 cm x d 17.2 cm
blown multilayered cane glass
with spiral threads
artist's collection

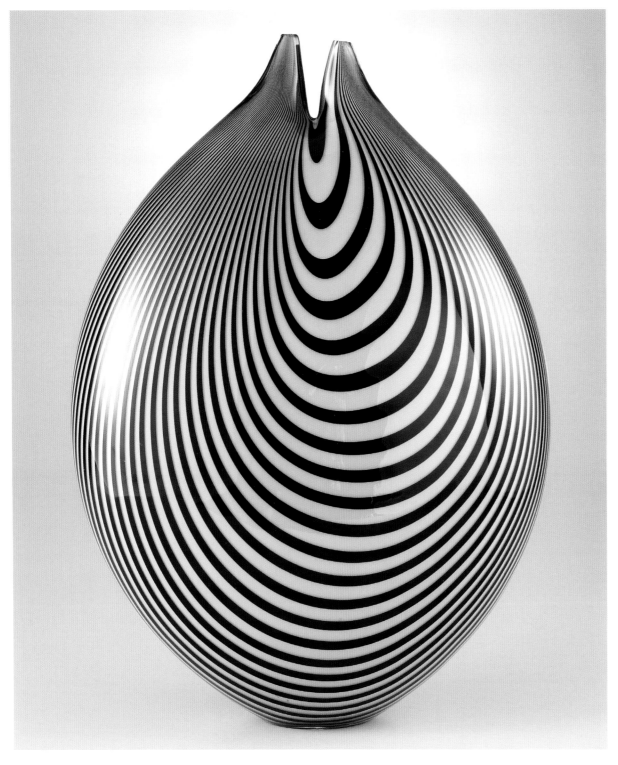

Two Sisters
1998 circa
h 39 cm x w 26 cm x d 14 cm
blown cane Pilchuck Ninety-Six
glass
artist's collection

Borneo
1999
h 45.7 cm x w 31.1 cm x d 21.6 cm
half-filigree blown glass
with applications of canes in relief
artist's collection

Provenza
1999
h 43.1 cm x w 34.9 cm x d 34.9 cm
'fabric' blown glass
artist's collection

Trullo
2000
h 40 cm x ⌀ 27 cm
blown cane glass, cold ground
then worked hot
artist's collection

Vase
2001
h 46 cm x w 26 cm x d 10 cm
glass in bands and polychrome patches,
blown, engraved and battuto
signed «Lino Tagliapietra 2001»
artist's collection

Seed
2000
h 65 cm
blown and battuto glass
Sandro Pezzoli collection, Milan

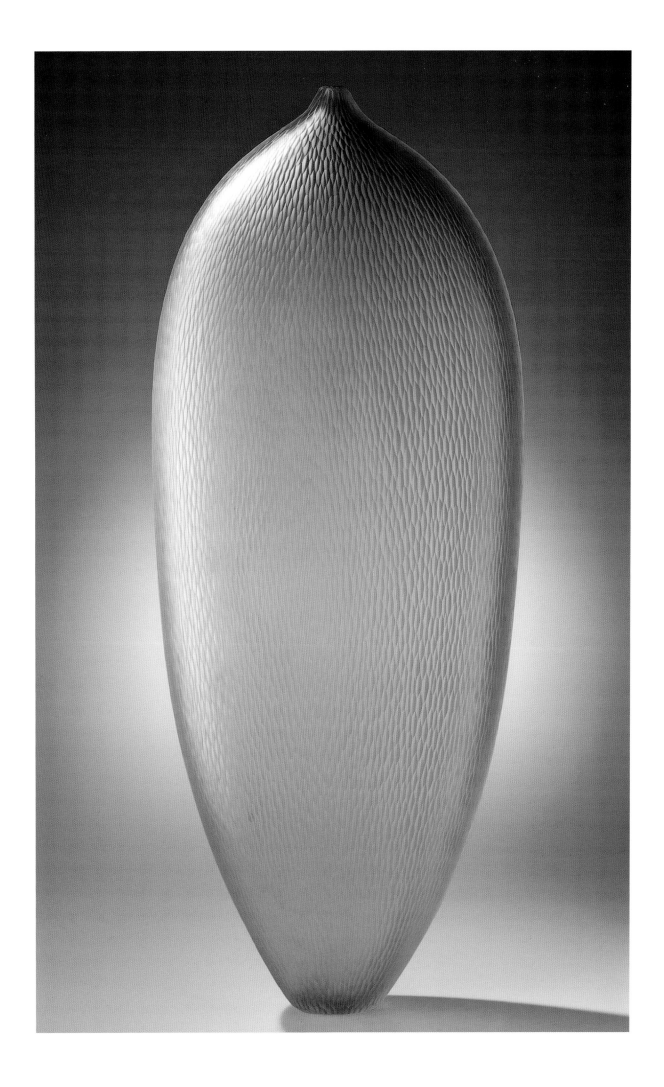

Foemina
2000
h 44.5 cm x w 31.1 cm x d 22.2 cm
blown cane glass, battuto
artist's collection

Silea
2001
h 63.5 cm x w 33 cm x d 22.2 cm
blown zanfirico cane glass
artist's collection

Batman
2003
h 28.6 cm x w 43.8 cm x d 8.3 cm
blown cane glass, ground
artist's collection

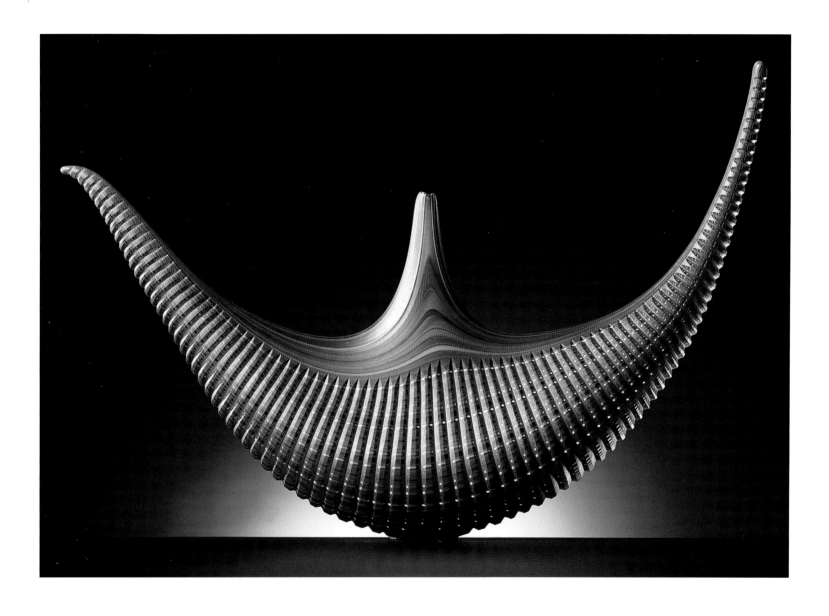

Hopi
2003
h 33 cm x w 39.3 cm x d 39.3 cm
blown cane glass, worked with
pincers
artist's collection

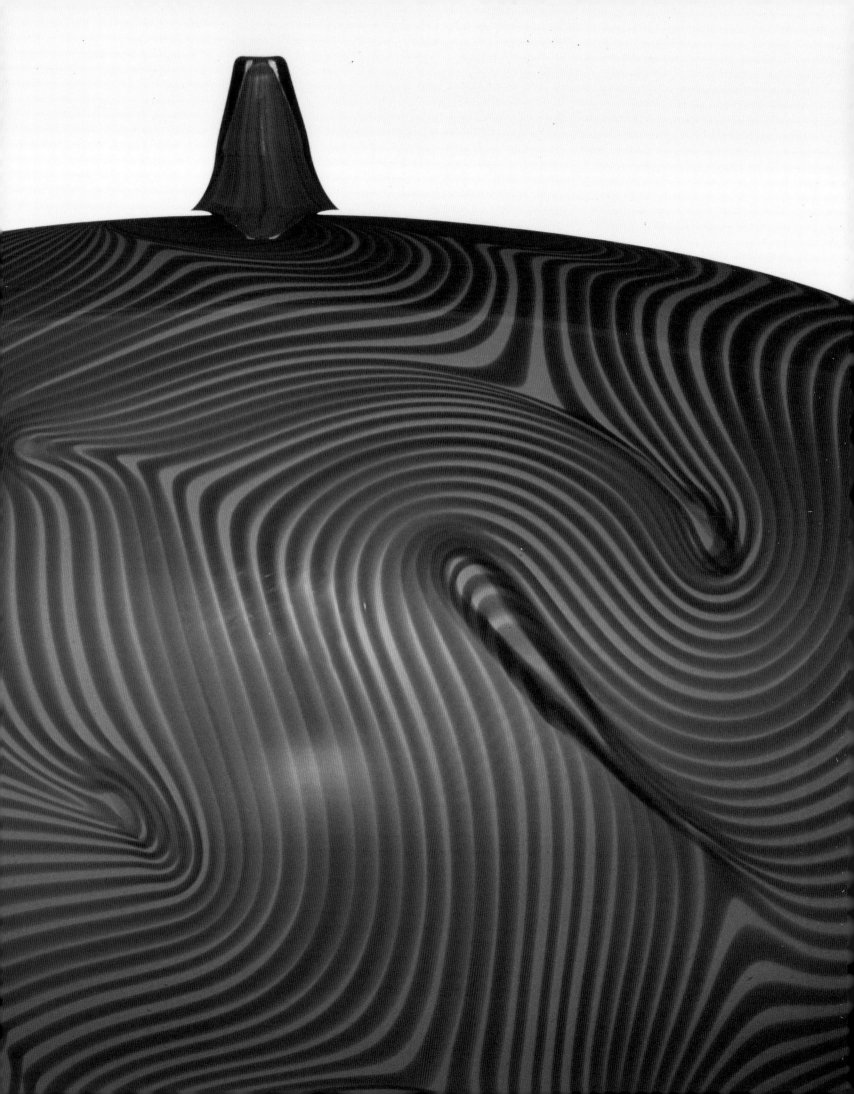

Fenice
2005
h 42.5 cm x w 47.6 cm x d 11.4 cm
blown cane glass, battuto
artist's collection

Mandara
2006
h 86.4 cm x w 39.3 cm
x d 17.1 cm
blown incalmo and half-filigree
glass, battuto
artist's collection

Stromboli
1996
h 20 cm x w 41 cm
blown murrine and cane glass
signed «Lino Tagliapietra»
private collection

Bilbao
2005
h 76.8 cm x w 21 cm x d 10.8 cm
blown incalmo and half-filigree
glass
artist's collection

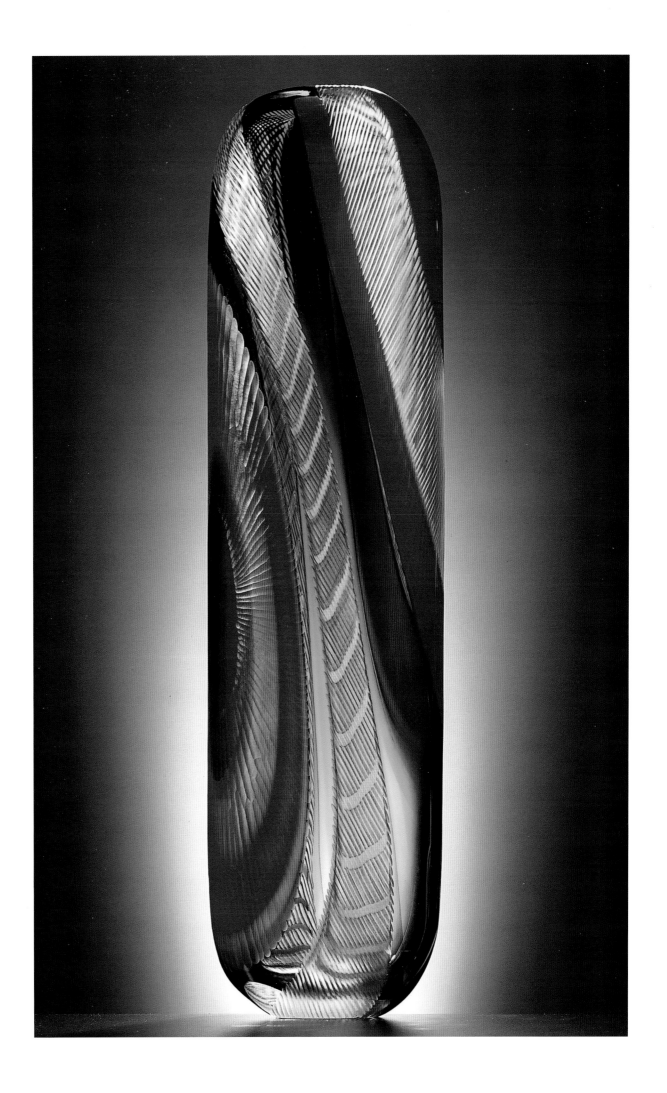

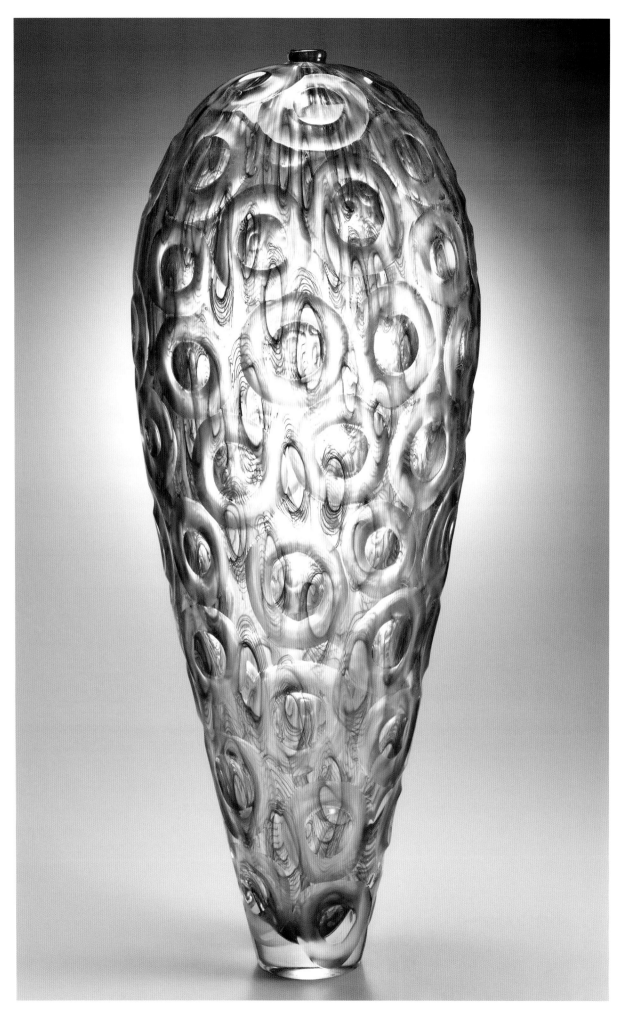

Vase
2007
h 49 cm x ⌀ 18 cm
blown glass with fragments of
twisted filigree, ground
artist's collection

Borneo
2007
h 53 cm x ⌀ 32 cm
half-filigree blown glass
with applications of canes in relief
private collection

Asola
2007
h 43.8 x w 35.6 cm x 17.1 cm
filigree blown glass
artist's collection

Makah
2007
h 41.3 cm x w 41.9 cm x d 31.8 cm
filigree tesserae blown glass
artist's collection

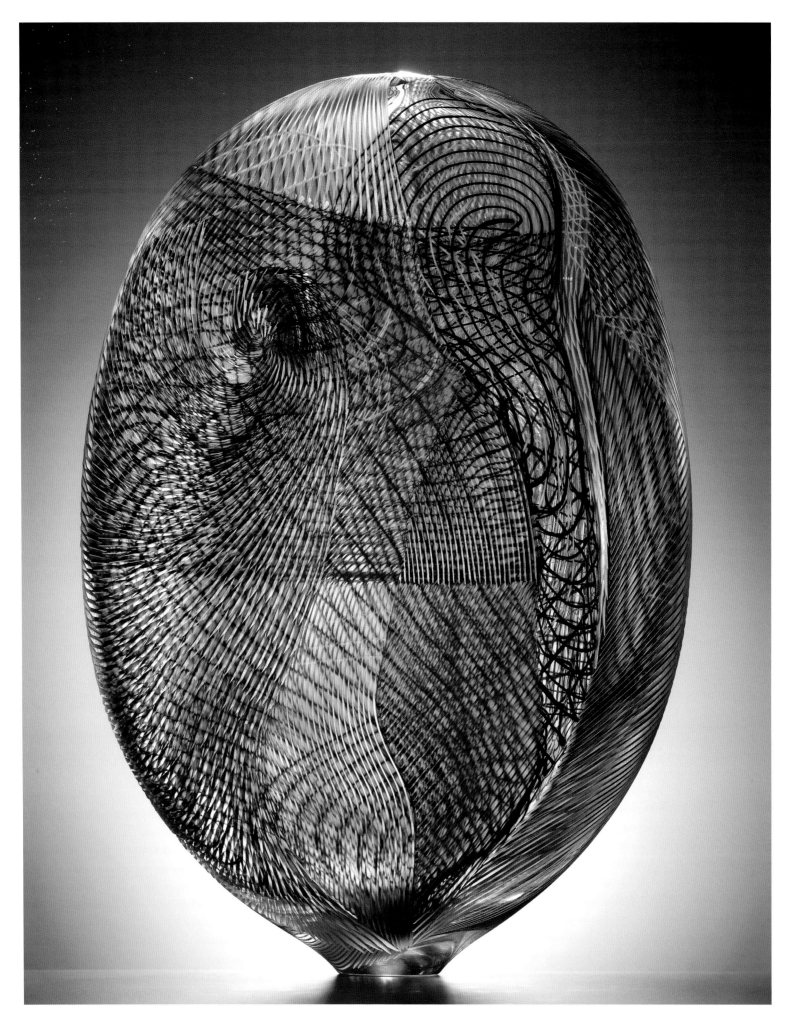

Ostuni
2008
h 53.3 cm x w 37.5 cm x d 13.3 cm
filigree and incalmo blown glass
artist's collection

Anto
2008
h 30.5 cm x w 29.2 cm x d 15.2 cm
blown glass with twisted ribbons
artist's collection

Chioccíola
2008
h 39.4 cm x w 36.2 cm x d 36.2 cm
blown glass with zanifico
segments
artist's collection

Piccadilly
2008
h 44.5 cm x w 42.5 cm x d 42.5 cm
half-filigree and incalmo blown
glass
artist's collection

Dada
2008
h 38.7 cm x w 34.9 cm x w 17.1 cm
blown glass with horizontal and
vertical incalmi, filigree, battuto,
hot application of cords
artist's collection

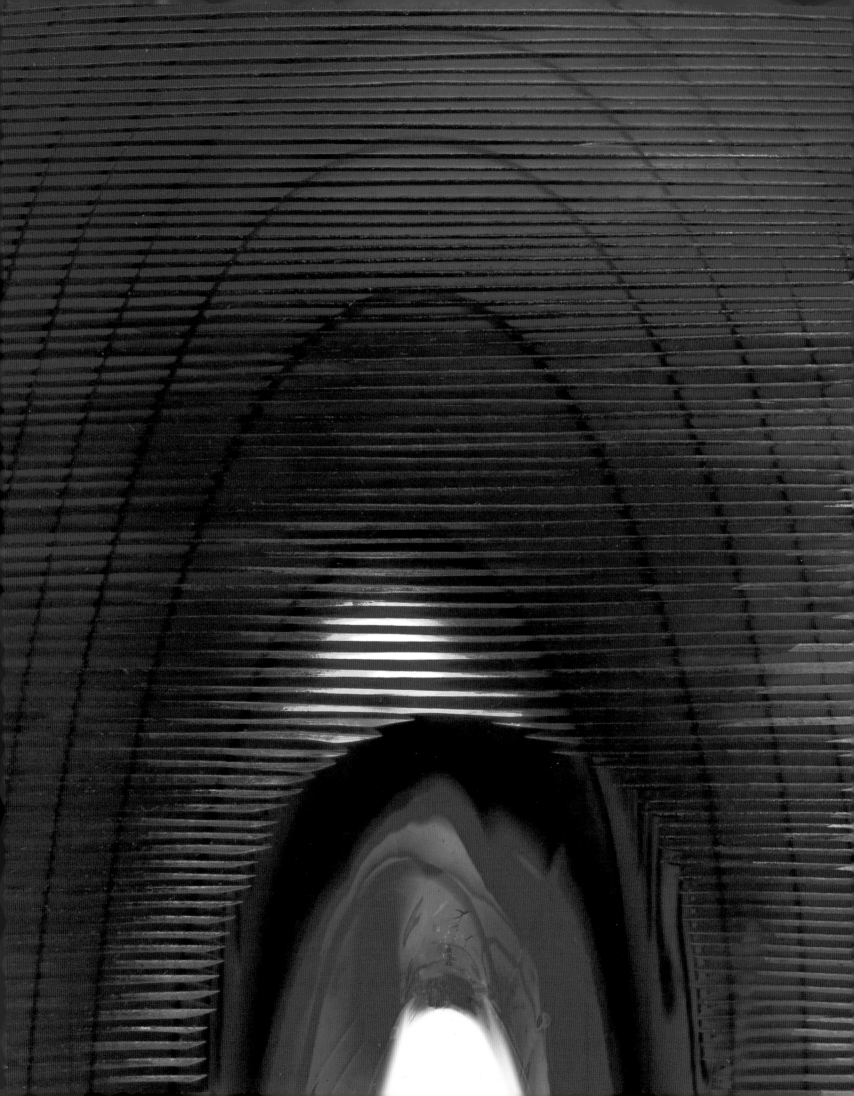

Morgana
2008
h 43.2 cm x w 22.9 cm
x d 8.9 cm
overlaid blown glass, engraved
artist's collection

Oca
2009
h 98.4 cm x w 24.8 cm
x d 19 cm
blown cane glass, incalmo,
battuto
artist's collection

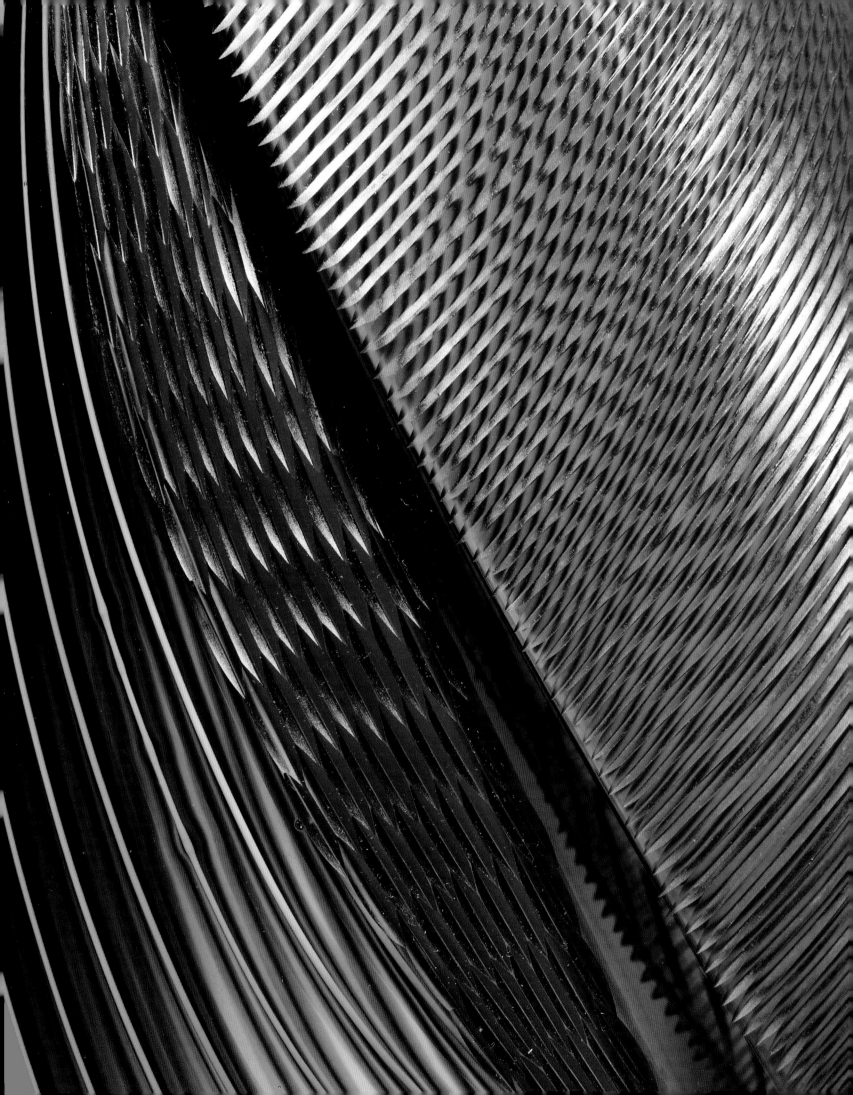

Edinburgo
2009
h 48.3 cm x w 41.3 cm x d 19.7 cm
filigree, reticello blown glass,
ground
artist's collection

Vienna
2009
h 61 cm x w 41.3 cm x d 21 cm
blown cane glass with
overlapping threads
artist's collection

Tatoosh
2009
h 67.3 cm x w 32.4 cm x d 20.3 cm
filigree blown glass
artist's collection

Seattle Sunset
2010
h 48 cm x w 42 cm x d 15 cm
filigree blown glass, battuto
artist's collection

Niomea
2010
h 71.8 cm x w 40.6 cm x d 19 cm
overlapping filigree blown glass
artist's collection

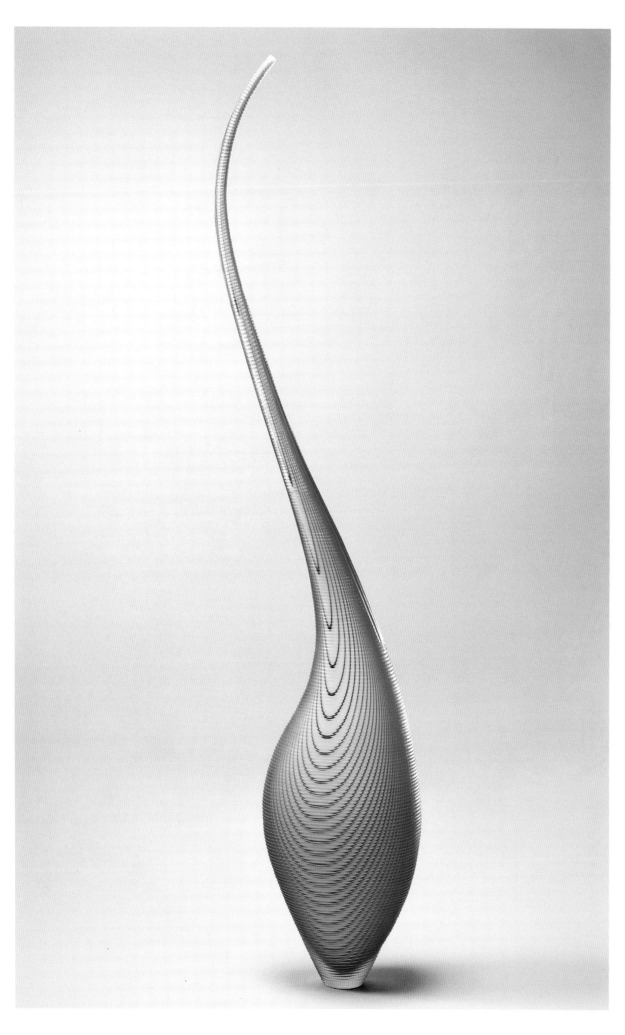

Dinosaur
2010
h 144.2 cm x w 34.3 cm
x d 16.5 cm
blown cane glass
artist's collection

Saba
2010
h 75.6 cm x w 45 cm x d 20.3 cm
filigree blown glass, ground
artist's collection

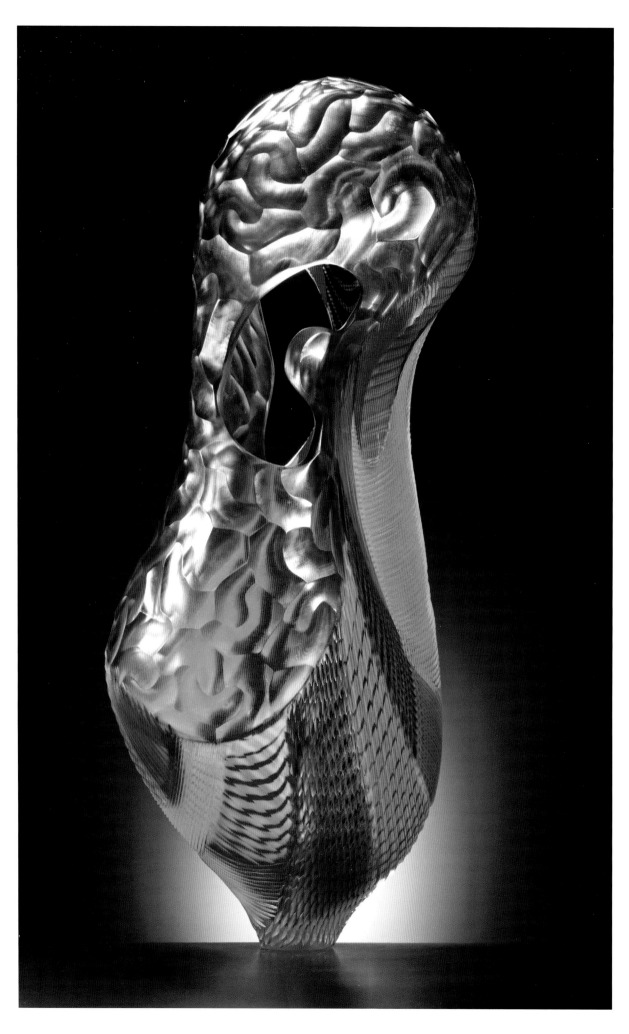

Bahia
2010
h 58.4 cm x w 26 cm
x d 26 cm
filigree blown glass, incalmo,
ground
artist's collection

Dinosaur
2011
h 154 cm x w 60.3 cm
x d 21.5 cm
half-filigree blown glass and
incalmi
artist's collection

Angel Tear
2011
h 85.7 cm x w 55.9 cm
x d 14 cm
half-filigree blown glass
artist's collection

Saturno
2011
h 68 cm x w 86.4 cm x d 17.8 cm
blown cane glass and incalmo
artist's collection

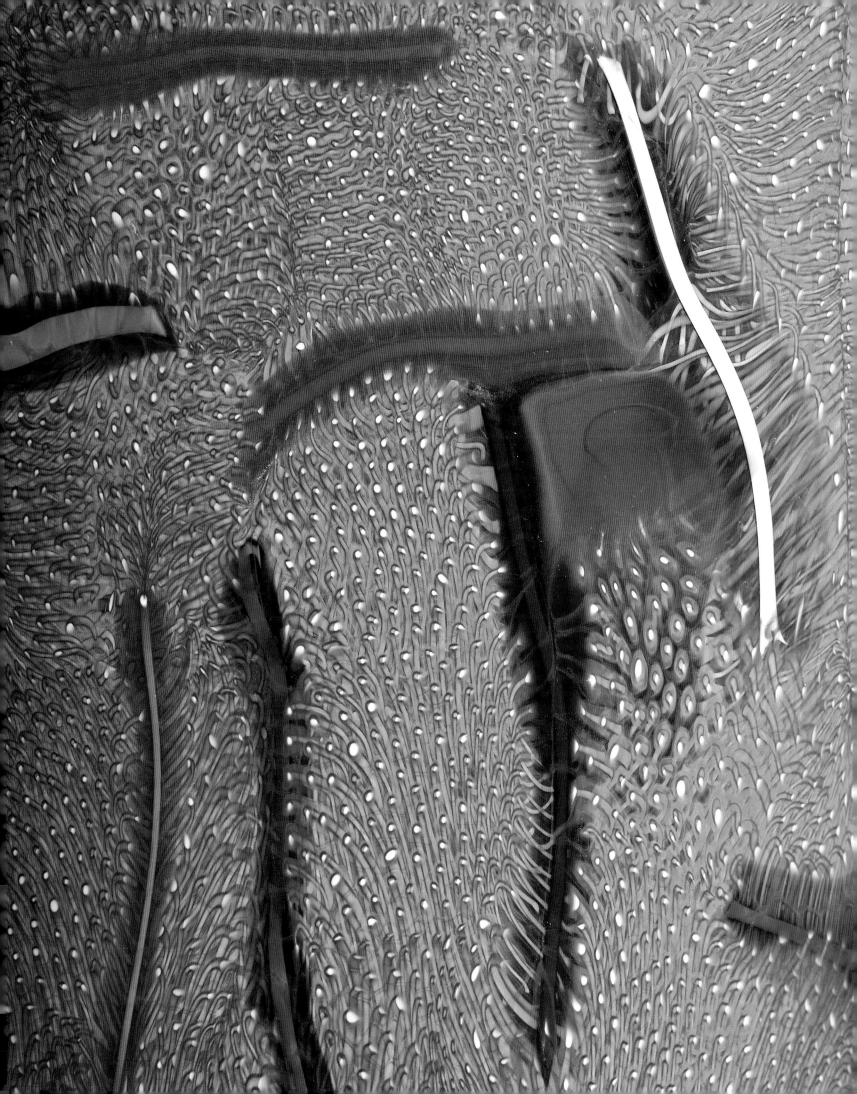

Osaka
2011
h 59 cm x w 27.9 cm
x d 27.3 cm
blown murrine glass
artist's collection

Fuji
2011
h 42.5 cm x w 48.8 cm x d 16.5 cm
blown murrine glass
artist's collection

Fuji
2011
h 52.7 cm x w 47 cm x d 26.5 cm
blown murrine glass
artist's collection

Endeavor
2011
h 220 cm x l 470 cm x d 180 cm
blown cane glass, battuto
artist's collection

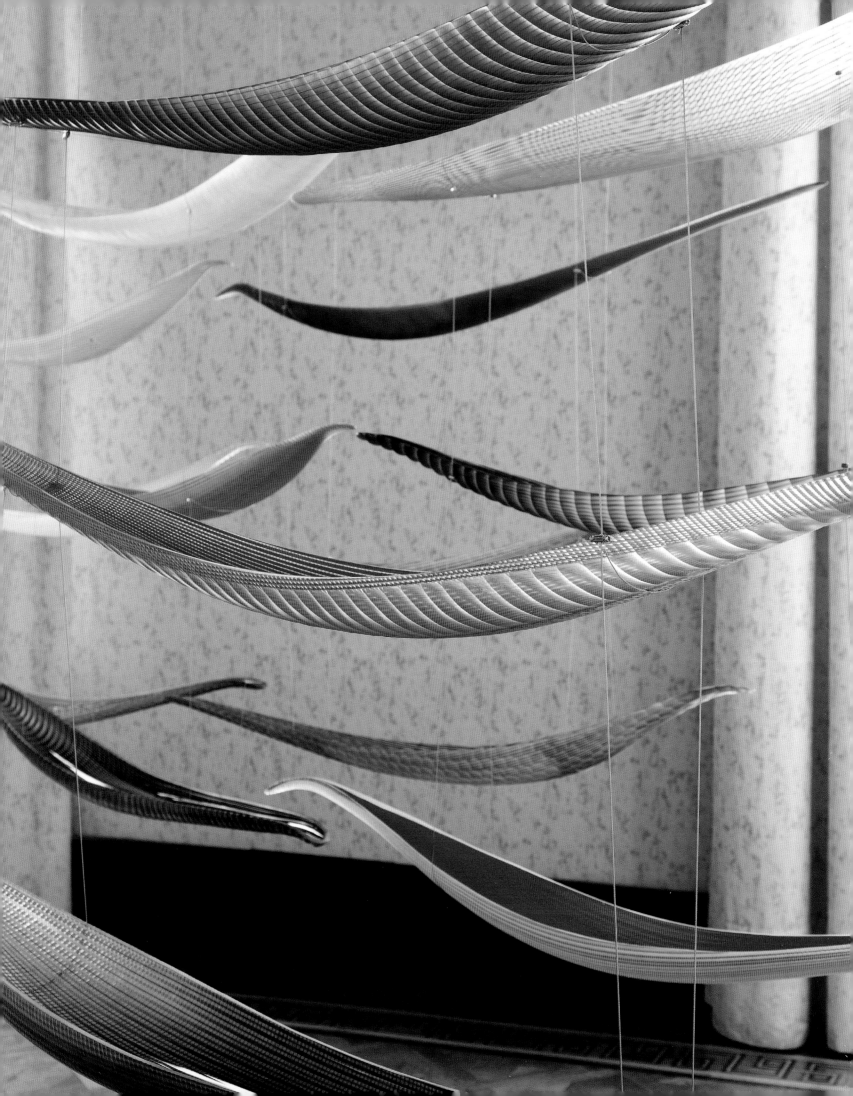

Gabbiani (Seagulls)
2011
h 300 cm x w 520 cm
x d 200 cm
blown cane glass, battuto
artist's collection

157

Masai
2011
h 150 cm x w 250 cm
x d 25 cm
blown glass, ground, gilt
artist's collection

Masai
2011
h 145 cm x w 185 cm
x d 23 cm
blown cane glass, battuto
artist's collection

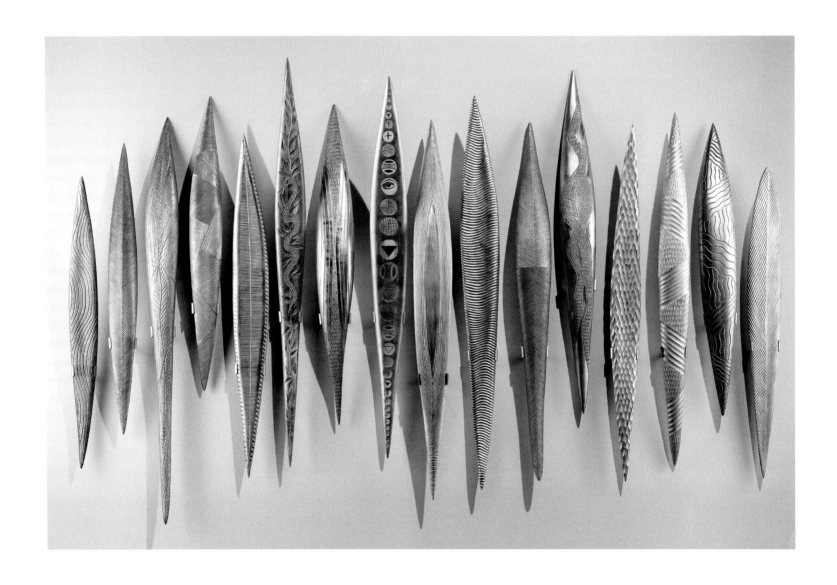

Avventura (Adventure)
2011
h 200 cm x w 102 cm
x d 14 cm
cabinet des merveilles
with 98 elements in
blown aventurine glass
artist's collection

Chronology

1926
Albino Tagliapietra (1896-1966) and Clementina Zane (1897-1990), Lino Tagliapietra's parents, move from Burano to Murano with their first-born son Silvano (1926-2003).

10 August 1934
Lino, Albino and Clementina's last child, is born in a house on the Rio dei Vetrai in Murano.

1945
Lino abandons his studies at the age of ten.

1946
Lino is employed as *garzonetto* to the maestro Attilio Frondi in the prestigious Vetreria Archimede Seguso, where he works until 1955, apart from the period of his military service (1952-1954).

1955
Already engaged to Lina Ongaro, he is employed as *servente* to Nane Ferro at the Vetreria Galliano Ferro owned by Galliano Ferro, the father of Silvano Tagliapietra's wife, Maria Antonietta 'Etta' Ferro.

1956
Lino becomes *maestrino*.

1957
Lino becomes *maestro*.

1959
Lino marries Lina Ongaro, daughter of a mosaicist from a venerable Murano glassmaking family.

1960
A daughter, Marina, is born; followed by Silvano (1962) and Bruno (1965).

1960
Lino makes some glass pieces designed by Giorgio Ferro for the Venice Biennale; and again in 1962.

1966
He makes some glass pieces to his own design. He leaves the Vetreria Galliano Ferro. At the end of the year he starts working as maestro at the Vetreria Venini, which he leaves in 1968.

1968
He is employed as primo maestro in the new La Murrina glassworks, where he begins designing objects and lamps for production. The *Saturno* presented at the Venice Biennale is made by him, developed from his own design, but not bearing his name.
He is awarded the Borselle d'Oro prize for excellence in the working of glass.

1972
He is awarded the Grand Prix at the Barcelona trade fair for the *Formichiere* lamp.

1975
He is awarded the honour of the Cavaliere dell'Ordine al Merito della Repubblica Italiana.

1976
He takes part in the First Course for Artists run by the Scuola Internazionale del Vetro.

1977
He leaves the La Murrina glassworks. He becomes *primo maestro* and artistic and technical director at the new Effetre International glassworks. Here he designs vases and lamps.

1978
He takes part in the Second Course for Artists run by the Scuola Internazionale del Vetro.

1979
He teaches for the first time at the Pilchuck Glass School in Stanwood, near Seattle, Washington. He later returns numerous times to Pilchuck to teach. He soon begins frequenting glassmaking studios in Seattle.

1981
He takes part in the Third Course for Artists run by the Scuola Internazionale del Vetro. On this occasion he meets Andries Dirk Copier (1901-1991) and works with him. They work together again in Murano and Holland through to 1990.

1982
His association with Marina Angelin begins, which will continue until 1986.

1987
He goes for the first time to the Haystack Mountain School of Crafts, Deer Isle, Maine.

1988
First important solo exhibition at the Museum Boymans, Van Beuningen in Rotterdam, Holland.
He is guest at the Centre International de Recerche sur Verre Plastique (CIRVA) in Marseilles, France.
He begins working at Dale Chihuly's Van de Kamp studio in Seattle on the production of the *Venetians*.

1989
He begins working with the artist Dan Dailey. He works with Dale Chihuly on the *Ikebana* series.

1990
He is invited to the major international exhibition *World Glass Now '94* at the Hokkaido Museum of Modern Art in Sapporo, Japan.

1991
He begins a casual working relationship at the Diaz de Santillana family's Eos glassworks, where he remains until 1993.

1993
He works with Dale Chihuly on the *Piccolo Venetians* series. He stops working with other artists and designers.

1994
The first monograph on his work is published: *Lino Tagliapietra: Vetri, Glass, Verres, Glas*, Giovanni Sarpellon (ed.), Venice 1994.

1996
He is one of the guests of honour at the *Aperto Vetro* exhibition in the Doge's Palace, Venice, where he exhibits the installation *Metamauco*. He is awarded the Rakow Commission for Excellence in Glass by the Corning Museum of Glass and the Urban Glass Award for the Preservation of Glassworking Techniques. Over the years he was to receive other important awards.

1998
He exhibits the installation *Flying Boats* at the second Aperto Vetro exhibition. He creates a collection at the Steuben glassworks in Corning.
He makes *La Carta dei Sogni*, a series of sheets in cast glass at Bullseye Glass in Portland, Oregon. The monograph *Tagliapietra: A Venetian Glass Maestro*, edited by Marino Barovier, is published in Dublin.

2000
The exhibition *A.D. Copier & Lino Tagliapietra: Inspiratie in glas, Inspiration in Glass* opens at the Gemeentemuseum, The Hague, Holland.

2004
He receives an honorary degree in Humane Letters from the Center College of Danville, Kentucky. He receives the President's Distinguished Artist Award, University of the Arts, Philadelphia, Pennsylvania; the Artist as Hero Award from the National Liberty Museum, Philadelphia; and the Artist Visionaries! Lifetime Achievement Award from the Museum of Arts and Design, New York City.

2006
He receives the Distinguished Educator Award from the James Renwick Alliance at the Smithsonian American Art Museum, Washington, DC.

2008
The Museum of Glass in Tacoma, Washington, opens the retrospective exhibition: *Lino Tagliapietra in Retrospect: A Modern Renaissance in Glass* curated by Susanne K. Frantz. In the years 2008-2010 the exhibition travels to other museums: the Smithsonian American Art Museum's Renwick Gallery, Washington D. C.; the Chrysler Museum of Art, Norfolk, Virginia; the Palm Springs Art Museum, Palm Springs, California; the Flint Institute of Arts, Flint, Minnesota.

Selected bibliography

Vetri Murano Oggi, exihibition catalogue (Venice, 1981), Milano 1981

Mille anni di arte del vetro a Venezia, Rosa Barovier Mentasti et al. (eds.), exihibition catalogue (Venice, 1982), Venezia 1982

Vetro di Murano: ieri ed oggi, exihibition catalogue (Tokyo and Nagoya, 1982), Milano 1982

Impronte del soffio: tradizione e nuovi percorsi nel vetro di Murano, Barbara Nerozzi (ed.), exihibition catalogue (Venice, 1987), Venezia 1987

Uit het licht van de lagune: textiel van Norelene; glas van Tagliapietra, exihibition catalogue (Rotterdam, 1988), Rotterdam 1988

Giuseppe Cappa, *L'Europe de l'art verrier: des precurseurs de l'Art nouveau a l'art actuel: 1850-1990*, Liège 1989

Susanne K. Frantz, *Contemporary Glass: A World Survey from The Corning Museum of Glass*, New York 1989

The Venetians: modern glass, 1919-1990, William Warmus (ed.), New York 1989

Natalie De Combray-Lino Tagliapietra, 'Conversation', in *Urban Glass Art Quarterly*, n. 39, 1990, pp. 12-13

Renee Maijer, *Lino Tagliapietra: Schatbewaarder van de Venetiaanse traditie*, degree thesis, Faculty of Arts, University of Leiden, 1990

World Glass Now '91, exihibition catalogue (Sapporo, 1991), Tokyo 1991

Rosa Barovier Mentasti, *Vetro veneziano 1890-1990*, Venezia 1992

Lino Tagliapietra: vetri, Giovanni Sarpellon (ed.), Venezia 1994

Vetri veneziani del '900. La collezione della Cassa di Risparmio di Venezia. Biennali 1930-1970, Rosa Barovier Mentasti (ed.), Venezia 1994

Maestri vetrai creatori di Murano del '900, Rosa Barovier Mentasti (ed.), exihibition catalogue (Comacchio, 1995), Milano 1995

Venezia Aperto Vetro - International New Glass, Attilia Dorigato, Dan Klein (eds.), exihibition catalogue (Venice, 1996), Venezia 1996

Glass, Vetro, Glas: Dale Chihuly, Lino Tagliapietra, Bertil Vallien, exihibition catalogue (Venice, 1996), Venezia 1996

Dan Klein, 'Lino Tagliapietra', in *Neues Glas - New Glass*, n. 2, 1996, pp. 26-33

Tina Oldknow, *Pilchuck: a glass school*, Seattle 1996

Lino Tagliapietra, exihibition catalogue (Ebeltoft, 1996), Ebeltoft 1996

The secret of Murano, Rosa Barovier Mentasti, Adriano Berengo (eds.), exihibition catalogue (Den Haag, 1997), Venezia, 1997

Tagliapietra: A Venetian glass maestro, Marino Barovier (ed.), Dublin 1998

Venezia Aperto Vetro - International New Glass, Attilia Dorigato, Dan Klein, Rosa Barovier Mentasti (eds.), exihibition catalogue (Venice, 1998), Milano 1998

Tina Oldknow, 'Conversazione con Lino Tagliapietra / Conversation with Lino Tagliapietra', in *Vetro*, n. 3, April-June. 1999, pp. 24-33

Titus M. Eliens, *A.D. Copier & Lino Tagliapietra: inspiratie in glas*, exihibition catalogue (Den Haag, 2000), Den Haag 2000

Glassway. Le stanze del vetro, Rosa Barover Mentasti et al. (eds.), exihibition catalogue (Aosta, 2002), Milano/Ginevra 2002

Concerto in glass: the art of Lino Tagliapietra, exihibition catalogue (Columbus, 2003), Columbus 2003

Vetri. Nel mondo. Oggi. Esposizione internazionale d'arte, Rosa Barovier Mentasti (ed.), exihibition catalogue (Venice, 2004), Sommacampagna 2004

Coburg Glass Prize for contemporary glass in Europe 2006, Klaus Weschenfelder (ed.), exihibition catalogue (Coburg, 2006), Coburg 2006

Susanne K. Frantz, *Lino Tagliapietra. In retrospect. A modern Renaissance in Murano glass*, Tacoma/Seattle/London 2008

Artisti e designer del vetro 1960-2010. La collezione Bellini-Pezzoli, Rosa Barovier Mentasti, Sandro Pezzoli, Cristina Tonini (eds.), exihibition catalogue (Milan, 2010), Venezia 2010

Photolitography
Fotolito Veneta, San Martino Buonalbergo (VR)

Printed by
Grafiche Nardin, Ca' Savio-Cavallino-Treporti (VE)
for Marsilio Editori® s.p.a., Venice

edition

10   9   8   7   6   5   4   3   2   1

year

2011   2012   2013   2014   2015